DON'T
Keep Me
a Secret!

Proven Tactics to Get More Referrals and Introductions

Bill Cates

McGRAW-HILL
New York   Chicago   San Francisco
Lisbon   London   Madrid   Mexico City
Milan   New Delhi   San Juan   Seoul
Singapore   Sydney   Toronto

The McGraw·Hill Companies

1 2 3 4 5 6 7 8 9 0   FGR/FGR   0 9 8 7

ISBN-13: 978-0-07-149454-0
ISBN-10:   0-07-149454-5

McGraw-Hill books are available at special quantity discounts to use as premiums and sales promotions, or for use in corporate training programs. For more information, please write to the Director of Special Sales, Professional Publishing, McGraw-Hill, Two Penn Plaza, New York, NY 10121-2298. Or contact your local bookstore.

This book is printed on acid-free paper.

Library of Congress Cataloging-in-Publication Data

Cates, W. R. (William R.)
  Don't keep me a secret / by Bill Cates.
     p. cm.
  ISBN 0-07-149454-5 (alk. paper)
  1. Business referrals. I. Title.
HF5438.25.C366 2008
658.8—dc22   2007008992

To my daughter, Jenna,
and to my sister, Linda, and her family:
Jessica, Kris, and Lee

Contents

Foreword

Referrals. Every salesperson and small business owner knows that referrals are the lifeblood of successful sales. The more referrals one gets, the easier everything becomes—closing ratios soar, profitability goes up, and the process is simply more enjoyable. Just about every top producer in every industry has created a referral-based business.

Top financial advisors work almost exclusively from referrals and generate personal incomes of $500,000 and more. Top car salespeople don't wait around for the "ups" (people to walk into the showroom); they're working their clients for repeat and referral business. Top real estate agents don't have to advertise much and certainly don't cold call in neighborhoods passing out flower seeds (like the rookies do). They work from referrals. Pick an industry and you'll find the same thing.

But most likely you've picked up this book because you probably already know this. The problem is that *most* salespeople and small business owners don't know how to generate referrals. They don't have a systematic approach to making referrals happen on a regular basis.

As the founder and publisher of *Selling Power* magazine (now in its twenty-fifth year), I've seen just about everything under the sun when it comes to selling strategies and tactics. But surprisingly, there's been very little work done in the area of how to generate referrals.

Most of the work on creating referrals has been disappointingly shallow. We are told that we need to get referrals—we need to ask, we need to service our clients and customers better to create word of mouth, we need to network in our communities better—but that's about as far as it goes. Even the top sales authorities that I've had the pleasure of listening to don't really teach how to create a steady stream of great referrals. Until now.

I don't say this lightly. Bill Cates is truly a master of the referral process. His first book, *Get More Referrals Now!* (McGraw-Hill, 2004), laid out Cates's system clearly and in a way you can act on to produce great results. Since Cates wrote this highly practical and superbly tactical book (which I highly recommend you read), he has taught his system to over 30,000 sales professionals and small business owners. And during that time—as you would hope and expect—Cates picked up many new ideas and best practices from sales practitioners. Cates's insights have evolved just as the marketplace has evolved. *Don't Keep Me a Secret!* is a superb compilation of these best practices, new ideas, and new tactics that people—just like you—are actually using successfully to generate more sales.

What I like best about *Don't Keep Me a Secret!* is the practicality and universal adaptability of his ideas. This is not a theoretical work. This is like an owner's manual on making referrals happen for you. Cates tells you what to do, how to do it, and why you should do it a certain way. All you need to do is adjust it slightly to your sales world and your personality—and then have the courage to act.

I dare you to read this book and not come away with a dozen or more ideas you can put to use immediately. And if you really do put them to use, you *will* increase your sales.

And . . . don't keep this great book a secret! Share it with everyone on your sales team. It may be against company policy to keep these best-practice ideas to yourself.

Gerhard Gschwandtner
Founder and Publisher, *Selling Power* magazine

Acknowledgments

I have been fortunate to be able to surround myself with supportive and capable people. Their actions and attitudes have contributed to my efforts to complete this book. To name a few: Willie Jolley, Steven Gaffney, Joel Rosenberg, John Hurley, Randy Richie, Jay Magenheim, Les Picker, Karen Hood, Deborah Ager, Jennifer Kreitzer, Sharon Landesberg, Dave Kelly, and Nido Qubein.

PART 1

PREPARE YOURSELF FOR REFERRAL SUCCESS

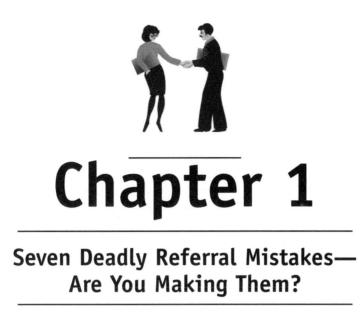

Chapter 1

Seven Deadly Referral Mistakes— Are You Making Them?

Most salespeople and small business owners don't get enough referrals, and you need to know the main reasons why. Once you're aware of this information, you should be able to get more from this book, and most important, put more of the ideas into action.

MISTAKE #1—LACK OF COMMITMENT TO REFERRALS

Are you committed to building a referral-based business? Really? Or are you just giving lip service to the notion? Sure, you may have the best of intentions, but your commitment shows through your actions—nothing else. Do your actions demonstrate a real commitment to making referrals happen for you?

Why are most people not fully committed to being proactive with referrals? Simple! It's fear. We'll go into more detail on this referral wrecker later, but fear is most often the root cause. The beautiful thing is that once you understand, face, and move through your fear, a whole new world of referral opportunity opens up to you. Your referral results increase substantially.

Here's a thought for you: how would your next great (best-ever) client prefer to meet you? Through a cold call? No! In a prospecting seminar? Only by default. From a direct mail piece? You've got to be kidding! Study after study has demonstrated that the best clients want to meet you through an introduction from someone they already trust, like a friend, family member, colleague, or advisor. Given this, why would you make referrals a passive process?

Student of the Game

Have you heard the expression "become a student of the game"? You hear this a lot in sports, where a player, who has become a student of the game, is able to become a great coach later in his or her career. A scholar is often referred to as a "student of history." I consider myself a "student of referrals." I am always learning from the people I teach. I read, listen to, and watch every referral educational program I can get my hands on. Why? Because the more I know, the better I can help you!

You too can become a student of referrals. Learn all you can—from me and from others. *Give* referrals so you know what it's like to be on the giving side of referrals. When you study referrals more—and actually *act* on what you learn—your commitment to building a thriving referral-based business will become even stronger.

MISTAKE #2—MAKING REFERRALS ALL ABOUT YOU

Perhaps you've heard this old method of asking for referrals: "Let me tell you how I get paid. I get paid in two ways. First I get paid a commission if you buy a product from me. Second,

I get paid in referrals. If you like the work I've done for you, then I'll ask you to refer me to others." Let me be perfectly clear about one thing. Stop saying this! Let's take a look at this approach for a second.

I think you already know that not everyone likes to give referrals. No matter how referable you are, some people just don't play the game. So, let's say you're in the presence of a new prospect or even a new client—a client who doesn't like to give referrals or who doesn't like to take the time to participate in referrals. Then you tell her this is how you get paid! You set referrals up as an obligation and not an earned right. Now tell me. Do you think you are *building* or *losing* rapport and trust?

Okay, I know that some folks still produce results with a producer-centered methodology. Heck, I used to teach a producer-centered approach! Although it can produce some results, even in today's marketplace, there is a far better way—better for your clients and better for you.

Use a *client-centered* approach to asking for referrals. Make it all about the value you bring to the clients and the value they recognize. Think about it this way: have you ever gotten a referral without asking for it? I sure hope so. Why would a client volunteer a referral to you? Simple. It's because she saw the value in the work you've done for her and wanted to introduce that value to others. Perhaps she wants to help you become more successful too, but that's secondary motivation. Clients give referrals *only* when they see the value in the work you do. So make your request for referrals all about your value and extending that value to others.

MISTAKE #3—FORGETTING TO ASK FOR REFERRALS

Do you ever forget to ask for referrals? Shame on you! If you're making this mistake, then you're clearly missing some huge opportunities to be introduced to some great clients. But are you *really* forgetting? Or is something else going on there?

I submit that what may really be happening is that you don't feel comfortable asking your clients for referrals so—unconsciously—you make little decisions along the way that sabotage your referral efforts. Only you know if this is true for you. I can tell you with great confidence that I know it's true for many salespeople and small business owners.

So, what do you do to fix this mistake? First, you need to truly commit to building a referral-based business—as I've already said. Second, you need to get yourself a "prop." Many producers are having great success using a referral journal to collect their referrals. They have a small black book (or whatever color you like) that they put out on the table during all, or most, of their meetings. This referral journal acts as a constant reminder (or prop) to do all the things I'm going to teach you in this book, such as plant referral seeds, hold value discussions, and ask for referrals. With this method, you don't forget—and therefore you manage your appointments much better.

Using the referral journal technique doesn't mean you have to ask for referrals on every appointment; it just means you won't forget. Now, when you do ask and you begin to get some referrals, open the journal and use it to collect your referrals. This validates the process for your clients and treats the request with importance.

If you'd like to see a great referral journal, check out the one on our Web site at www.referralcoach.com. Our introductions journal not only will serve you as mentioned above but also will prompt you to ask certain questions of your referral sources to increase the quality of your referrals and introductions.

MISTAKE #4—NOT BEING REFERABLE IN THE FIRST PLACE

Being referable is a critical component to generating referrals. In fact, you can't get referrals without being referable. Are you referable? How do you know? Well, one barometer of your referability is if you're getting referrals without asking for them. Are you? Every business and every sales professional should be getting referrals without asking for them. Regardless of the exact nature of your business, there are people out there who like to give referrals. You should at least be getting those.

Unfortunately, these *passive* referrals aren't usually plentiful enough or are not always the right match for your business. This is why we want to find ways to be proactive—as much as possible—without being pushy or obnoxious.

So how do you become more referable? With prospects and new clients, it's all about the process you go through with them. It's *not* about your products. Having great products certainly helps, but the greatest product in the world won't cause a client to give referrals to you if your process is not referable. Sure, the client may brag about the product, but not about you. Think process, not products.

Now, what keeps you referable over the lifetime of your client relationships? There are three levels of activity you must engage in to ensure that your clients continue to refer you:

1. *Transactional.* You must have systems, standards, and staff in place to make sure you don't drop the ball and to ensure that all transactional aspects of your practice are handled with impeccable service.

2. *Value added.* If you don't continue to add value to your client relationships, then you are no longer necessary. Think of all the possible ways you can bring more value to your clients. Being realistic, bring as much as you

can to your "A" clients. Bring a subset of that to your "B" clients, and a subset of that to your "C" clients.

3. *Business friendships.* Build as many business friendships with your clients as possible. Some may not want to be your business friend and you may not want to be business friends with some of your clients. But in most cases, this is a desired outcome with your clients. People do business with their business friends and they refer business to their business friends. One of the best ways is to host a client appreciation event such as a wine and cheese party or an evening at a baseball game. When you get to know your clients in venues outside your normal business environment, it's much easier to create business friendships.

MISTAKE #5—THINKING GREAT SERVICE ALONE IS ENOUGH

Many people operate under the illusion that "if I just serve the heck out of my clients, they will refer me to others." Well . . . some will. But many more won't unless you nudge the process along and become proactive, which is what this book is all about. You'll learn so many different ways to nudge your referral process that you'll have no excuses left for not engaging in it.

MISTAKE #6—LETTING YOUR FEAR GET IN YOUR WAY

Why don't most folks ask for referrals? You already know the answer. I told you in Mistake #1, it's fear. Let's go a little deeper into that now.

I've heard just about every reason in the world for why people don't ask for referrals. While the exact words change with each individual, every reason I've ever heard is based on fear. The good news is that at the core of each fear is the solution to that fear. I'll give you a couple of examples. You'll get the point.

Fear #1—Asking for referrals will make me look unsuccessful. I don't want to beg for referrals. Of course you don't want to reduce yourself to begging—no one does. But can you see how this attitude is fear based? "I don't want to ask for referrals because I *fear* being judged as unsuccessful by my clients." So what's the solution to this fear? Simple. Find a way to ask for referrals that comes from a position of strength, that comes from a place of confidence, abundance, and success. Make it all about the value you bring to others and the confidence you have in your ability to help people. This is what our Unlimited Referrals® Marketing System teaches. It's a client-centered approach to referrals that's all about strength and nothing about weakness or begging. It's a system that actually works!

Fear #2—Asking clients for referrals will hurt my relationship with them. No it won't! Not if you ask in the right way; one that simply doesn't hurt relationships. When you use a client-centered approach that is a bit softer than what has historically been taught, you'll never hurt a relationship. For years, the way salespeople have been taught to ask for referrals has been an aggressive approach. It has, in my opinion, polluted the waters for us. Many of us—including our clients—have had a bad experience with someone being aggressive with referrals. Perhaps you are keenly aware of this and have vowed to not show up like that. The problem is that you err too far in the other direction and don't ask at all. The good news is that if you use our VIPS Method™ (see Chapter 5), you will not come across as pushy or aggressive. This softer approach is still effective, but never hurts a relationship. Using the VIPS Method™, one of three things will happen and one thing will never happen: (1) some clients will give you referrals when you ask;

(2) some won't give you referrals when you ask, but they'll give you referrals later; and (3) some won't ever give you referrals. However, you'll *never* hurt the relationship.

What's your fear? What's your barrier? Figure that out and you'll find the solution.

MISTAKE #7—NOT USING A SYSTEMATIC APPROACH

How can you expect to build a thriving referral-based business if you're only dabbling in referrals? Sure, you know what to do with a referral when you trip over one, but to create referral momentum, you need to employ a systematic approach on a regular basis.

It's like playing pool or billiards. In billiards, as you're trying to make a particular shot, you're also looking ahead to your next shot. You're trying to leave your cue ball in a position that will set up your next move. In billiards, if you're any good, one shot will lead to the next.

That's what you want to do with your referral process. You bring prospects into your office, or you go to theirs, and you convert them into clients. That's good. But if you don't have a simple referral process in place, then what happens? Do you have to get back on the phone and make cold calls or call expensive leads that don't seem much better than cold calls? Do you have to gear up to do another seminar or another direct mail piece? Or maybe you just wait around for your next referral? That would be a shame! Making sure you have a referral process in place is vital.

With a referral process in place—which you employ on a regular basis—you bring prospects into your sphere of influence and convert them into clients in such a way that they become not only clients but also leads to other people. The good news about referrals is that one client can lead to two, and two can lead to four, and four can lead to eight. With a steady referral process in place, your business grows exponentially. My first book, *Get More Referrals Now!* (McGraw-Hill, 2004), goes into much more depth on how to create a truly systematic approach. That book will also give you the elements of the system.

So there you have it: the seven deadly referral sins. Are there really more than seven? You bet there are. But these are some of the key ones for you to examine for yourself.

Chapter 2

What's in It for You?

Since you're reading this book, you probably already know some of the benefits of getting more referrals and building a thriving referral-based business. But I want to make sure you get the full picture. I want to make sure you get excited about what the ideas in this book will help you achieve. Listed below are some of the perks you'll enjoy when you make the commitment to build a strong referral-based business.

NO MORE COLD CALL HELL

If you've ever had to make a lot of cold calls to get your sales going, then you know exactly what I'm talking about here. Okay, there are a few strange birds who actually like to cold call (telephone or in person), but they are few and far between. I've done my fair share of cold calling over the years. While I believe that any salesperson or small business owner worth his or her salt should always be willing and able to get on the phone and call strangers, the good news is that except for a start-up business or sales career, it just isn't the best way to build a business.

IT'S EASIER FOR YOU TO GET APPOINTMENTS AND EASIER TO MAKE THE SALE

Since cold calling is a pure numbers game (with a high dose of luck thrown in), the ratio of calls to appointments is usually pretty low. Working from referrals always yields a significantly higher call-to-appointment ratio and appointment-to-sale ratio. You are starting off the relationship at a higher point of trust than in any other form of marketing, so appointments are always easier to secure and sales are easier to confirm.

YOUR SALES CYCLE IS SHORTER

Every business has a normal sales cycle. Some large or more complicated sales usually take longer to consummate than smaller sales do. But whatever the normal sales cycle is for your business, you can rest assured that working from referrals will, on average, shorten that cycle. Why? First, because you enter the relationship at a higher level of trust—sometimes being the only one bidding on the business. Second, you are often referred at just the right moment, when the need for your product or service is at a hot point.

YOUR COST PER LEAD APPROACHES ZERO

All businesses need to be concerned with their cost per lead. In other words, what does it cost you or your business, through advertising, mailings, telemarketing, and/or promotional materials, to generate each new qualified prospect? In many businesses, the cost per lead is often hundreds or even thousands of dollars. Now, what does it cost to generate a great referral? How about zero? Nada! Okay, maybe a small thank-you gift to the referral source, but that's about it.

YOUR SALES ARE LARGER

I've seen a number of studies in the life insurance industry that demonstrate that the size of the average sale to a referral client is often twice as much as the average sale to a client generated by other means. Twice as much! So, working from referrals means you can spend less time selling and still make more money.

YOUR BUSINESS IS MORE PROFITABLE

With your cost per lead decreasing, your average sale increasing, and your overall marketing budget decreasing, your business will be more profitable. If you own the business, that means more money in your pocket. If you don't own the business, it makes you a more successful and more valuable sales rep.

One company I worked with had an annual telemarketing budget of over $400,000. Its cost per lead was between $300 and $500. That put a lot of pressure on the sales force and ate away at the profit margin. The company hired us to train its salespeople in our referral system and help them build a solid referral culture. Then the company fired its telemarketing firm.

Now, you might think the company's sales would suffer for a bit, but the lower cost per lead might slightly offset that. The truth is, the company's sales actually increased. In fact, in the first full year without telemarketing it broke every sales record it kept. The company had a banner year—and without the $400,000 drag on its profitability.

YOUR SELLING PROCESS IS MORE ENJOYABLE

When you work from referrals, you're meeting your prospects the way they want to meet you—from a recommendation or introduction, from someone they trust. You borrow that trust long enough to earn your own trust. So you will have not only a higher closing rate, larger sales, and all the benefits I've already mentioned, but you will also have more fun in the selling process. The higher trust and higher comfort level coming from your prospects equals a smoother, more enjoyable process.

YOUR CLIENTS ARE MORE LOYAL

I've seen at least two studies that demonstrate that clients who come into your business through referrals remain your clients longer. Since your prospects enter into a relationship with you at a higher level of trust, you can build on that trust even more quickly. (I'll show you how to do so in Chapter 3.) Also, when they are referred to your business by one of your current clients, they now know at least one other person who does business with you. This works to continually validate their decision to go with you.

YOUR CLIENTS ARE 2½ TIMES MORE LIKELY TO GIVE YOU REFERRALS

Did you know that the clients you bring into your business are more likely to give you referrals? It makes sense. Since they were introduced to you by someone they trust, they already understand the dynamics of meeting you from a referral.

What can happen over time is that a critical mass of referred clients gets created and the referral process begins to take on a life of its own. Eventually, you can create so much referral momentum that all you need to do is take great care of your clients and you'll never lack for new business.

YOU'RE LIVING A REFERRAL LIFESTYLE

There is no better place to be in sales and marketing than in a "referral lifestyle." As mentioned above, all your new clients are coming to you from strong referrals—the place where you no longer have to chase after prospects. This is also where your sales are the size you want and at the profitability you want, and where the energy you have to put into sales and marketing becomes effortless and fun. I suggest that this be your goal—to live a referral lifestyle.

BUT WAIT! THERE'S MORE

The great thing about the referral process is that you are not the only one who benefits. Your clients benefit in a number of ways: their decision to use you is validated, they get a chance to help others, they get better attention from you, and they enjoy helping you succeed. Plus, your new prospects and clients benefit from meeting you through a referral. They feel more comfortable with you from the start, and they get the great value of your processes, products, and services. The referral process has multiple winners!

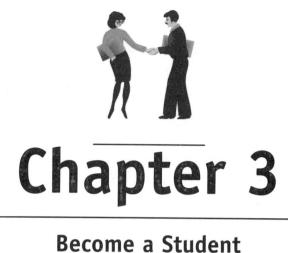

Chapter 3

Become a Student of the Referral Game

Most salespeople and small business owners dabble in referrals. I'm sure you know what to do with a referral or introduction if you stumble over one. But do you have a systematic process to make referrals and introductions commonplace in your business? Your journey to building a thriving referral-based business begins with your commitment to doing so. And I don't just mean a commitment of lip service or a commitment of wishing and hoping. I'm talking about a commitment of *action*!

DO YOU HAVE A REFERRAL MINDSET?

The desire to get your clients to not keep you a secret begins with putting forth some serious thinking and awareness. Powerful thinking translates into powerful (and effective) actions; and the more effective your actions, the better your results. I call this having a referral mindset. What's your mindset? Listed below are examples of a referral mindset.

1. *You realize that your best prospects would prefer to meet you through a referral above any other way.* This realization will enable you to make referrals your primary method of prospecting. In other words, you've made a full and complete commitment to building a referral-based business, and your actions are consistent with that high-level commitment.

2. *You're tapping into the lifetime value of your clients.* You stay in contact with your clients, not just to maintain loyalty, but also to leverage that loyalty into a lifetime of referrals. You see, most people think the lifetime value of clients is merely the business you can do with them over a lifetime. However, there is also the value of referrals you can get from them during that same period of time.

   Over the years I've had the opportunity to interview many extremely successful salespeople and small business owners. If there's one common denominator or theme that comes out of all these conversations, it can be summed up in just three little words: "Work your book." Work your book of existing businesses; serve them well so they stay with you; learn about them and educate them so they can do even more business with you; and get introductions from them when the timing is right. Ask yourself, "Who is it easier to sell something to, a new prospect or an existing client?" Work your book and tap into the lifetime value of your clients.

3. *You have and use the system for generating referrals rather than leaving it to chance.* One sad truth I discovered when I started teaching the Unlimited Referrals® Marketing System many years ago was that most salespeople and small business owners *dabble* in referrals. But in order to truly generate more sales, you have to

use a systematic approach, and use it on a regular basis. This book will give you that system, but, of course, it's up to you to actually use it.

You see, it's like billiards. If you've ever played billiards, you know what this is like. I'm aiming the cue ball to hit the number 4 ball into the side pocket. But I'm also trying to do something else at the same time. I want to leave the cue ball in position to hit the number 7 ball into the corner pocket. In billiards, one shot leads to the next.

And this is precisely why you want to have a referral system in place. You bring prospects into your world and you turn them into clients. You make the shot. And that's great. But what happens if you don't have a system in place to get referrals? Do you have to wait for the next prospects to contact you? Do you have to do another expensive and inefficient mailing?

With a referral process in place, one client can lead to two (or more), two clients lead to four, four clients lead to eight, and so on. By using referrals, your business can grow geometrically. In case math wasn't one of your strong subjects, that means *fast*.

4. *You are always connecting people by giving referrals.* There is no faster way to start getting referrals than by giving referrals. Are you a referral giver? Are you connecting people in all sorts of ways? Perhaps some of your clients could be doing business with each other. Perhaps you have other resources your clients should know about.

Have you heard the expression "become a student of the game"? It's something you often hear in sports. When a player is described as being a student of the game it means he or she really understands the game.

That person is often described as being a good candidate to become a coach or manager. I'd like you to become a student of the game. Learn all you can about how and why referrals work for you and for others.

One great way to be a student of referrals is by giving referrals. You'll see how many people benefit from this process. You'll also see the risks sometimes associated with giving referrals. Knowing these will allow you to become better at helping your clients give referrals by minimizing their perceived risks.

One more thing to realize is that if you are a reluctant referral giver, it could be sabotaging your desire to get more referrals. Start making great connections for others, and they'll do the same for you.

5. *You expect to get referrals.* Your attitude of expectation creates more powerful awareness and action. Would you agree with this next statement? "Going into any situation with an attitude of expectation increases the chances of that thing happening." Of course, it doesn't guarantee a result, but it increases the chances.

I call this having "confident awareness." First, you're confident about the work that you do. You have confidence in your products and services and in your own ability. Second, you have an awareness of all the opportunity that's right in front of you on a regular basis. This confident awareness, or attitude of expectation, will lead to more powerful action on your part.

After teaching my system for over 12 years, it has become quite clear to me that the most important ingredient in building your referral-based business is your referral mindset—your day-in and day-out awareness and commitment to action.

NOT A PROCESS TO SELL, BUT A PROCESS TO BRING VALUE

Would you like to get referrals sooner in your relationships? Would you like to get quality referrals from prospects? The key to doing so is to bring real value to your relationships in the very first appointment.

Most companies with which I work have processes to move the sale along: "Five Steps to Closing the Sale," "Seven Steps to Consultative Selling," and so on. And that's fine. I believe that every small business owner and salesperson should have a process for moving the sale along and getting the order.

However, very few companies with which I work have a process that's expressly designed to move the sale along by providing value to the prospects. In over 25 years of selling, I've learned that when you provide tangible value early in the relationship, not only are you more likely to make the sale but also you'll do it in a way that will make you referable very early on. You won't have to wait days, weeks, or months to become referable.

Here are four things you can do to become as referable as possible very early in the relationship:

1. *Think "process," not products.* Don't just have a process to "make the sale." Have a repeatable process to bring "tangible value." The last thing you want to be is an "order taker." Sometimes you bring value by creating big-picture thinking so that the service you give your clients isn't performed in a vacuum. Sometimes you can provide value by teaching them not just about your product or service but also about how to buy your product or service. And, if you have the courage, you can provide value by questioning their assumptions about you and what you sell.

2. *Learn as much as you can about the prospect.* Be genuinely curious. Be a good listener. Do this before you make any recommendations. You may have already heard the phrase "prescription before diagnosis is malpractice." Not only is this statement true for medicine, it's true for sales as well.

3. *Always be ready to give referrals.* Connect prospects and clients with other professionals who might be of service to them. Also, learn about who makes a good prospect for them and try to refer businesses to them as well.

4. *Be on time for all appointments, do what you say you will do, and finish what you start.* These thing should be a "given." Sadly, too many salespeople and small business owners show up late (without a call ahead), don't always do what they said they would, and don't always finish. Bottom line: no surprises!

IT'S ALL ABOUT TRUST

Throughout this book, you'll hear me talk about the importance of trust in the referral process. I believe that the level of trust needed to make the sale is not necessarily the level of trust needed to get referrals. We must constantly work on building higher levels of trust with our prospects and clients. And trust is not an easy thing to build quickly.

Here's a very important point: you can't force trust. Using gimmicky sales techniques won't win trust; only sincerity and truth win it. With that said, here are a few dos and don'ts for building trust with your prospects and clients:

Don't

1. Be arrogant, cocky, or self-serving.
2. Reveal proprietary information about other businesses.

3. Tell off-color jokes or curse.

4. Talk badly about your competitors or other clients.

5. Interrupt or monopolize conversations.

6. Show up late.

7. Ignore or sit on problems.

Do

1. Let your confidence in yourself and your product or service show through.

2. Discuss your prospects' and clients' expectations for the relationship.

3. Type up and send those expectations back to your clients in a letter or an e-mail to demonstrate you were listening and understanding.

4. Listen intently, taking notes when appropriate.

5. Keep your word; do what you say you will do when you say you will do it.

6. Be flexible in your communication style, adapting it to the style of your prospect or client.

7. Fix problems quickly and to your clients' satisfaction; admit it when you've made a mistake—that's often the most important part.

8. Always tell the truth, even when it feels uncomfortable or may cost you a sale.

EXPERTS GET REFERRED

Do your clients view you as an expert in your field? When they think of you, do they think: "He really knows his stuff. He's head and shoulders above the rest"? When your clients perceive you as a true expert, their egos get involved. They want others to know that they are "working with the best."

How can you become perceived as an expert? Here are four ways:

1. Learn as much about your product, service, industry, or whatever as you possibly can. Truly gain more knowledge than most of your competitors.

2. Get published. Submit articles to magazines and newspapers. You can start with the small local publications and then work your way up. Write a pamphlet, booklet, or full-fledged book.

3. Speak to groups in your area of expertise. You can speak to prospects to gain new business and you can add value to your current clients by speaking to them.

4. Become a specialist. Don't try to be all things to all people. Narrow your focus. Deepen your knowledge. Become the preeminent expert in a narrow field—as I like to think I have done with referrals.

THREE LEVELS OF NICHES TO BRING YOU RICHES

One truth I've discovered in business is that the more focused you become, the more successful you are. Targeting a market niche is a powerful strategy that few salespeople and small business owners adopt. Yet, it's one of the best ways to build a highly profitable business. There are three types or levels of niches for you to consider.

Level 1

This is the highest and best type of niche. Here, all or most of the members of your niche know one another in some way. They have formal and informal ways of communicating with one another. This would be something like owners of printing companies, restaurants, publishers, or physicians. It is quite easy to create a good reputation for yourself in a Level 1 niche.

Level 2

Here is where all the members of your niche have some very strong commonality but may not necessarily know many others like themselves. An example of this type of niche is divorced or widowed women. It takes a little longer to establish yourself (reputation) within this type of niche, but it can be done.

Level 3

Here, the commonality is even more general. It would be like targeting people in an age group; this level niche has some value, but it's tough to build your reputation with this sort of group. People who target this kind of niche quite often fall into product-focused relationships, which are not great for generating referrals. However, over time, because of the great expertise you build in this area, it can be effective—it just takes longer.

So, as you can see, a Level 1 niche is the best. Going after a niche makes it easier to get referrals for two main reasons: (1) you provide more value—real and perceived—to clients in your niche; and (2) they know people like themselves. The more value you bring, the more they spread your good word.

I was working with a printing company in the Midwest that had 12 salespeople. We had each salesperson pick an industry niche to focus on and begin building a reputation. It started a little slowly at first. However, by the end of that year, sales were up by 10 percent over the previous year. By the end of the following year, sales were up another 30 percent. Also, profitability went up. Competition on price went down somewhat, and the cost of acquiring a new customer went way down.

VAGUE INTENTIONS PRODUCE VAGUE RESULTS

Here's a sad fact I've observed over the years. Most salespeople and business owners don't really know who their ideal client is—whom they would really like to clone. Why? Probably because they just haven't taken the time to find out. I suggest—strongly—that you take the time. I once heard a wise man say, "Clear intentions produce clear results. Vague intentions produce vague results." This means that it's hard for you to attract the exact types of clients you want unless you are very clear on what you want.

Most business people walk around with a notion of who'd they like to attract to their businesses. But a notion has very little pulling power. Take the time to articulate—on paper—whom you serve the best and who serves your business the best (this should be one and the same type of client). Work with others in your company to get a very clear idea of who this client is.

Dan Sullivan is the founder and president of a wonderful entrepreneurial coaching program called the Strategic Coach (www.StrategicCoach.com). When I went through Dan's program, one powerful concept he taught was called "The Largest Check." In a nutshell, he had us identify the clients who spent the most money with our company. They might not write out the largest single check, but they spent the most money over a period of time. We then identified the quantitative and qualitative attributes of those clients. And then we explored how we could go about finding more just like them—and even better ones. It was a very powerful exercise. I now have a clear sense of who fits my business and who doesn't, and of who I really want to attract. Do you? If you don't, get working. It won't take very long, and you'll be glad you did.

ALWAYS COME FROM A PLACE OF ABUNDANCE AND NOT A PLACE OF NEED

With both sales and referrals it's always a good choice to approach clients and prospects from a place of abundance. What I mean by this is that when you're trying to make the sale, you can't come across to your prospect as though you *have* to make the sale. The same applies when you're asking for referrals; you can't come across as needing referrals. Your neediness will make your clients and prospects uncomfortable. When they feel uncomfortable with the process, the process usually breaks down.

You've probably heard the expression (or something similar) "concentrate on your labors and not the fruits of your labors." When it comes to selling and generating referrals, you want to focus on what is within your control, not on what is out of your control. You can control whether or not you ask for referrals. You cannot control whether or not a client will give you referrals. You can control whether you ask for the order. You cannot control what your prospect's response will be.

Now, I know it is easier to talk about this than to actually do it. If you are new in your business or experiencing a slow-down, you're not always aware of when you are projecting a sense of desperation. I know that in my own experience as a salesperson and small business owner, when I come to an encounter from a place of abundance (I don't need the business), I usually get the business. If you don't believe me, I urge you to talk to some of the most successful salespeople and small business owners you know about this concept.

PART 2

Tactics and Strategies to Get More Referrals

Chapter 4

Get Great Prospects Calling You

If you're not referable, you won't get referrals. It's as simple as that. You have to be referable in the eyes of your clients or they won't tell others about you. You have to be referable in the eyes of your centers of influence, referral alliances, and your friends and families, or they won't tell others about you.

This chapter gives you ideas, tips, and tactics to become more referable through the processes you use and the ongoing service your deliver. I know many businesses that have been able to generate a huge number of great referrals just by making their clients go "wow."

The bottom line to providing great service and forming great relationships is that you must truly care about your clients. You must be fully committed to delivering first-class products, processes, and services. You must want to do it. You—and everyone in your company—must have an attitude of service toward your clients. An attitude of service is almost impossible to teach. Either you have it or you don't. For referral marketing to work for you, you must strengthen your company's attitude of service.

WHAT DO YOUR CLIENTS THINK ABOUT YOU—REALLY?

If you're not getting as many referrals as you would like, you need to make sure you are referable. Are your clients truly satisfied in their relationships with you? Are you good enough to keep their business but not good enough to win their referrals? Do you really know what they're thinking?

One business study conducted at the Strategic Planning Institute in Cambridge, Pennsylvania, discovered that 96 percent of unhappy clients won't complain—especially about the little things. Yet, they also found that complainers are more loyal than noncomplainers. Most of your clients will not tell you exactly how they think and feel about doing business with you unless you ask them.

It's critical you give your clients ample opportunity to express what they think and feel about doing business with you. Take your clients' "satisfaction temperature" on a regular basis. Say something like, "On a scale of 1 to 10, where are we right now? Is there anything we could be doing to serve you better?"

I know that asking this type of question takes a lot of courage. It's not always easy to do so because you fear getting a negative response. But if you have clients who have been withholding some information they need to tell you, they could be harboring resentments. They are candidates who will move their businesses sooner or later, and they are surely not going to give you referrals.

Some companies like to send out a type of yearly written survey to their clients, and doing so is fine. But mailing surveys doesn't replace the face-to-face or ear-to-ear conversations you need to have with your clients. You *must* know where you stand with your clients. Don't let fear hold you back! Make direct conversation a habit.

TALK ABOUT EXPECTATIONS IN THE RELATIONSHIP

One critical ingredient in creating loyal clients and getting refer-rals from them is trust. In fact, you'll need to establish a higher level of trust to turn clients into advocates than you will to con-vert them from prospects into clients. If they don't trust how you'll handle their friends or colleagues, they won't refer you, and their loyalty could be tenuous at best. You need to do whatever you can to grow trusting relationships as quickly as possible—to earn their business and earn their referrals.

One way to do so—early on in your new relationships— is to talk about what they expect from you and your company. There are different ways to get into this conversation. Here are some examples:

> "If you could build the perfect financial advisors, what would they look like?"

> "If you could build the perfect bookkeeping service, what would it do for you?

> "Let's imagine it's three years from today. What needs to happen over those three years for you to feel that our relationship has been successful?

> "What does a successful working relationship between us look like?"

Now here's an important point: this can't just be technique you're using on your prospects or clients; you really have to care about the answer. When you ask this type of question, and you are genuine about it, two things will happen. First, you'll learn a lot about what your prospects or clients expect in their relationships with you. Having this knowledge will help you to deliver better service to them. Second, this conversation is a trust-building one. When you genuinely demonstrate your care for the future of your relationships, it builds trust. That, in turn, increases referability.

TAKE A LEADERSHIP ROLE

One way to bring more value to your relationships with clients is to take a leadership role with them. It's important that you allow your experience and confidence to positively impact your client relationships.

Here's a specific example. Mike Brown is an extremely successful financial professional. He's among the top of the top. He said this to me a few years ago:

> Our job is to transfer our belief in what we do to our clients. If we believe it, our clients are more likely to believe it. For instance, it took me two hours to convince the client of the importance of being financially secure in case of unforeseen events. Over two years later, my client was diagnosed with an inoperable brain tumor.

Now, do you think Mike's client thanked him for taking a leadership role in his life—making sure he had proper life insurance, disability insurance, long-term care insurance, and catastrophic illness insurance in place? You bet he did. Perhaps this is an extreme case. However, the concept applies to you no matter what you sell. Help people make the right decisions for themselves, their families, and their businesses.

It takes courage to question people's perspectives. The key to doing it is to make sure you really understand those perspectives before you share your own. If other people feel that you are truly listening to them, they will then be more open to your point of view.

DON'T FORCE YOUR CLIENTS TO YOUR COMPETITION

Are you fully tapping into the lifetime value of your clients, or are you handing your clients over to your competition without realizing it?

More than one study confirms what makes sense intuitively, that client retention increases with each additional product or service your client purchases from you. The banking industry has long known that if a customer of the bank has seven channels of business with the bank (for example, a checking account, a savings account, certificate of deposit, home equity loan, safe deposit box, mortgage, and consumer loan), that customer's lifetime loyalty is pretty much guaranteed.

A life insurance industry study conducted by an insurance association known as LIMRA (formerly known as the Life Insurance and Market Research Association) found that with financial advisors, insurance agents, and other industry professionals:

- One product sold to a client gives a 35 percent chance of retaining a client over five years
- Two products sold to a client gives a 56 percent chance of retaining a client over five years
- Three or more products sold to a client gives a 92 percent chance of retention over five years.

Here's an interesting study from the mortgage industry. Only 17 percent of mortgage clients used their last vendor. The biggest reason for this sad loss of business was the lack of a personal relationship between the client and the vendor.

First of all, I'm not advocating you try to sell things to your clients that they don't need and won't find valuable. You should always put your clients' needs first (or equal to your own). You should always strive to create win-win relationships. With that said, many a sale is lost by salespeople and small business owners who fail to recognize the full value of a client to their business. Client loyalty and referrals go hand in hand. A truly thriving referral-based business is hard to build when you don't intend to build client loyalty at the same time.

In the words of author and sales expert Kerry Johnson, "It's a self-supporting system. You need a good relationship to cross-sell the client, and cross-selling also fosters stronger bonds. So before you try to sell additional products to any client, make sure you've laid a strong foundation of personal connection and flawless service."

DO YOU HAVE A REFERRAL PERSONALITY?

When I talk about "being referable" I usually focus on the issues of the *value* you bring to prospects and clients, and the quality of the ongoing service you provide throughout the relationship. But there's another aspect of your referability. It's the elusive quality of "a referral personality"—meaning, do you behave in a way with your prospects and clients that makes them want to refer you to others?

In dealing with many salespeople and small business owners over the years—in our coaching program, boot camps, and the like—I have met many for whom my first reaction was: "I can see why this guy doesn't get any referrals." It is almost instantly obvious to me that he or she does not have a particularly "referable personality."

Usually these folks fall into two categories—sheep and wolves. They are either so meek that they do not portray confidence, or they are so overbearing that they push people away. The sad part—in both cases—is that they either don't realize this about themselves, or they are unwilling to change their behavior.

Below is a checklist of personality traits and behaviors that I suggest you use to gauge if you have a referable personality. But it really doesn't matter what *you* think. You're probably blind to many of these issues anyway. What matters is what *your clients* think. So, if you have the guts, run this checklist by some of your friends, colleagues, and even some close clients to see how they rate you on a scale of 1 to 5 (with 1 being low and 5 being high).

Trait	*Rating*				
1. Positive attitude	1	2	3	4	5
2. Pleasing tone of voice	1	2	3	4	5
3. Good listener	1	2	3	4	5
4. Proper volume of voice	1	2	3	4	5
5. Proper eye contact	1	2	3	4	5
6. Undistracted	1	2	3	4	5
7. Unrushed	1	2	3	4	5
8. Client centered	1	2	3	4	5
9. Appropriate wardrobe	1	2	3	4	5
10. Too thick of an accent	1	2	3	4	5
11. Exude confidence (but not arrogance)	1	2	3	4	5
12. Natural and personable	1	2	3	4	5
13. Exudes trust and integrity	1	2	3	4	5

TRUTH OR CONSEQUENCES

Why is it that so many salespeople, customer service people, business owners—heck, just about everyone—have trouble telling the truth? I don't mean always out-and-out lying. I mean the constant withholding of important information, telling half the story, or fudging the truth in some way. The answer is simple. It's fear. Fear that by somehow telling the truth, the client will get angry and the relationship will be hurt—perhaps forever.

One thing I've learned through owning several businesses and selling for several years is that "the truth shall set you free!" The more I've been forthcoming with the truth, the whole truth, and nothing but the truth, the better my client relationships have become. Of course, you never want to out-and-out lie to a client. On the same note, you and everyone you work with must make sure that you are not afraid to deliver bad news to your clients. If you do it correctly, most of your clients will actually respect you for it and trust will build—and so will your referability.

BE CAREFUL ABOUT MAKING ASSUMPTIONS

How many times have you gotten off the phone or left the presence of a prospect or client and settled for a "fuzzy phrase" or incomplete answer—wishing you had probed or clarified just a bit more? Sometimes it takes a little courage, but I don't think you should take what your clients say at face value. You shouldn't assume you understand. Take the time to clarify.

When clients say they need something "as soon as possible," stop and find out exactly what "as soon as possible" means to them. When clients say "we want the highest quality," do you know what "highest quality" means to them? When an internal client (someone with whom you work) says "I'll try," get that person to make a time-frame commitment.

When you accept vague phrases from your internal clients, it makes it harder for you to serve your external clients. Client service suffers. The same is true for your regular clients. Accepting fuzzy phrases not only can lead to diminished service, it can also cause big problems.

THANKS FOR THE BUSINESS

Almost every businessperson knows about the value of sending a handwritten thank-you note after making a sale or performing a service. Yet most businesspeople are not in the habit of doing this. This gesture alone will help you to stand out in a crowded marketplace. How many thank-you notes did you send out last year? Send out twice as many this year.

And I'm not talking about an e-mail "thank you." I'm talking about a handwritten note, mailed in a hand-addressed envelope with a real stamp. Want to add a fun touch to this? Include a scratch-off lottery ticket. If your client is out of state, include a statement that you'll be happy to help cash in the winning ticket. We just did this with our holiday cards. Not only did our clients enjoy the fun touch, many of them won a little bit of money.

One of the best ways to thank clients for their business is with client appreciation events (see Chapter 5 for more about these activities). And a powerful subset of client appreciation events includes events where you invite only those clients who have given you referrals. Now you're thanking them for their business and their referrals.

You can show how you appreciate your clients in many other ways besides thank-you notes. Many salespeople and business owners like to keep a steady stream of ad specialties flowing to their clients: mugs, pens, sticky-notes, and the like. I suggest you look for even more creative ways to use ad specialties as part of your appreciation mix. After all, something with your logo on it is not really a gift. It's an ad for your business.

My friend and mentor Nido Qubein, president of High Point University in North Carolina, calls this "a trail of tangibles,"and he's the master at sending his clients tangible items. Some of them have real value, and some of them are just plain fun. At the university, Qubein has applied what he's learned as a successful businessman. For instance, when he first arrived at High Point, he had a kiosk built in the middle of campus to provide free soda and other beverages (no, not beer and wine) to the students. This was a simple thing that the students really appreciated. He then gave to all the students t-shirts that said "High Point University—Meet Me at the Kiosk." Of course, this was something that only a High Point student understood. However, Qubein knew that most of the students would wear these t-shirts while at home during their breaks. Their friends would ask them, "What does 'meet me at the Kiosk' mean?" The students would tell their friends about the free soda at the kiosk and about the ice cream truck with free ice cream. Then the friends would say, "Your school gives you free soda? Free ice cream? Wow, that sounds like a great place!" This is a concrete example of how a trail of tangibles creates referrals and word of mouth.

AN AGE-OLD CLIENT LOYALTY BUILDER

Doing something special for a client's birthday is an age-old client loyalty builder. Are you doing something special for your "A" clients' birthdays? Here are a few ideas:

1. Send birthday cards to your clients—personally signed by you and your staff. Make sure the cards are hand addressed and have real stamps on them.
2. Call your clients on their birthdays. Sing to them, if you dare. This will get you maximum impact.
3. Deliver birthday cakes, edible fruit arrangements, or other "flashy" items.

4. Host birthday parties for them and some of their friends.

5. Have champagne delivered to their homes or offices. Make a splash! Do more than others would do!

6. Buy them gifts. You don't have to spend much if you tailor the gifts to their personal interests or hobbies. We sent a really cool gift to a client recently. He's a huge Boston Red Sox fan, and we found a great gift on the team's Web site—a photo of a player crossing home plate, being greeted by other players (like he just hit a home run). What made this present even better is that we were able to customize the name of the home-run hitter with our client's last name. Now, don't you think this will be hung in his office? Do you think people will say, "Where did you get that?"

7. Go to the Web site www.dmarie.com/timecap and get a snapshot of things that happened on your clients' birthdays throughout history—songs, prices of things, level of the Dow Jones Industrial Average, famous people born on that day, and so on. You can print these "reports" and send them as gifts. I like this idea because it achieves more of the personal connection you want to create.

CALL YOUR CLIENTS WITH GOOD NEWS

Depending on your business, you may have opportunities to call your clients between the time they place the order for a product or service and when you deliver it. Get in the habit of scheduling one or more status report calls (or e-mails) to let your clients know that everything is on schedule. They will appreciate you checking on their order or project. And everyone appreciates a "good news" call.

SEVEN IDEAS TO CREATE "WOW" AND MORE REFERRALS

Here are a few ideas that folks who sell use to create the "wow" factor with their clients. They build business friendships that lead to more referrals. Use the ones that fit your business model and leave the rest.

1. *Birthday lunch.* Call clients two to three weeks before their birthdays and offer to take them and two to three of their friends to lunch. The dining place doesn't have to be an expensive one. They'll appreciate something "nice enough" but convenient to their offices.

2. *Valentine's Day.* I was coaching a financial advisor who, every year, hosts a Valentine's Lunch for all his female clients. He makes this a lunch in case these ladies have plans and so that he can take his wife out for dinner that evening. He says he nets several new clients each year just from the lunch, and then several more later in the year from the goodwill he's created.

3. *Business cards.* Print business cards for your retired clients. They no longer have business cards, but they could probably use them from time to time. You can put a graphic on them that reflects one of their hobbies.

4. *Singles events.* Host events just for singles—clients and their referrals. Do it more than once per year—maybe quarterly if it really starts working. You can introduce yourself very briefly at each event, but the rest of the time is just for fun.

5. *High Tea.* Invite women to a "High Tea" at a fancy hotel. I guess you can invite men too, but this sort of thing is usually a "ladies type of thing." Either way, it's novel and can lead to some great, fun conversation.

6. *Resource center.* Give all your clients' the names of certified public accountants, attorneys, auto body shops, car repair shops, house painters, HVAC (heating, ventilating, air-conditioning) specialists, plumbers, handymen (who actually return your call and show up on time)—you name it. Pay attention to people who do good work and stand by it. Be a resource for your clients. The more they call you for help, the better for you!

7. *Hand car wash.* When a very high-level client is in your office, make arrangements to have your assistant take the car out for a hand car wash. You don't do this for everyone. You don't have time, and it costs some money. However, depending on your business, think of the "wow" impact this could have when used strategically. Heck, I like it when I take my car into the Lexus dealer and they wash it for me. I wouldn't be surprised if many of your clients would want to visit you if you get their car cleaned too.

SOMETIMES THE LITTLE THINGS ARE THE BIG THINGS

Here's a list of little things you can do for clients that can go a long way toward increasing your referability.

- *Stretch.* If you paint houses for a living and your client needs the name of a good roofer, find him one. If he is staying at your hotel and his car gets a flat, change it. Help your client. What things can you do that won't make you any money—directly—but will add to your clients' experience of you?

- *Nickel and dime.* Don't charge for "extra" services when you don't really need to. Take an inventory of all the products and services you provide to your clients. What are a few things you could surprise your clients with by saying "no charge"? Don't worry. You'll more than make up the money in future business and referrals.

- *Workin' 9 to 5.* Don't just be there for them from nine to five. Handwrite your cell phone number on your business card as you give it to them. They'll likely never use it unless they really need to, but it reassures them.

- *Keep your word.* Doing what you're supposed to do, when you are supposed to do it, is the very minimum required to provide good client service and get referrals.

- *Say "I'm sorry!"* When something goes wrong, and it will, apologize to your clients. When you apologize, you're not admitting fault, you're just expressing that you're sorry they were inconvenienced. It reduces tension because it demonstrates you are there for them. (Almost no one in business ever says he or she is sorry.) Then, immediately after you apologize, fix the problem as quickly as possible.

- *Set the bar high.* Set high service standards for yourself and your company. And tell your clients—doing so will hold you accountable to them.

- *Don't burn bridges.* If clients stop doing business with you, don't burn your bridges. Go out of your way to make them feel comfortable about coming back. Then, when their new service provider drops the ball, they know you'll welcome them back.

- *Compromise with a smile.* If you have decided to give clients what they want, even if doing so is not a win for you, give in completely and cheerfully. Don't make clients feel guilty. Guilt doesn't create loyalty or engender trust.

- *Maximize satisfaction.* Help your clients understand your business. Teach them the best ways and times to interact with your business to maximize their satisfaction. Explain your systems and why they are best for them as well as for you. When you let your clients into some of the inner workings of your business, they often feel special. They like that.

- *Thank you!* Say "thank you" every time you get the chance. Enough said.

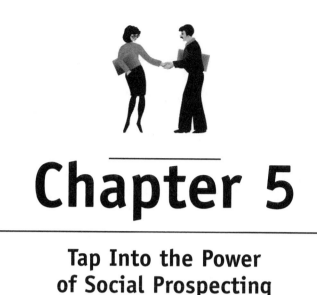

Chapter 5

Tap Into the Power of Social Prospecting

Social prospecting is the use of social venues and opportunities to identify, meet, and grow relationships with qualified prospects for your business. With the advent of the National Do Not Call Registry, the popularity and effectiveness of social prospecting has grown significantly. Whether you sell directly to consumers or to other businesses, you should make social prospecting part of your marketing mix.

There are many prospects for your business who would love to have the opportunity to meet you in a social setting before meeting you in a business setting where they know they may be asked to commit to a decision. For both parties, social venues are a good way to "test the waters" with regard to personality match.

CLIENT APPRECIATION EVENTS

I'd like to draw a distinction between what are called client appreciation events and referral events. In a nutshell, a *client appreciation event* is some sort of social gathering (fancy or informal) with the sole purpose of saying "thank you" to a client. A *referral event*, while the basic activity can be the same, the purpose is for one or more of your clients to invite one or more prospects to meet you.

Client appreciation events allow you to take your client relationships into new directions and to new levels that probably wouldn't be possible through the normal course of business events. You get to know each other in new ways. From this comes an expanded appreciation for each. This dynamic not only enhances client loyalty but also makes you more referable. People give referrals to people they like and trust. Client appreciation events contribute significantly to that dynamic.

TYPES OF CLIENT APPRECIATION EVENTS

The size and type of client appreciation events can vary greatly. In fact, I recommend you host a variety of such events each year. Not all of your clients have the same interests, so you don't want to leave anyone out. Also, smaller events allow you to spend a lot more time with your clients rather than being spread too thin. Some types of events lend themselves to more interaction than others. Make sure you build in plenty of time for interaction. For instance, if you invite several of your clients to the theater, make sure you have time built in on the front or back end for everyone to socialize.

Here is a list of a few of the types of client appreciation events that I've seen work:

- Holiday parties
- Picnics
- Sporting events
- Wine and cheese tastings

- Chocolate tastings
- Intimate fancy dinners
- Golf outings
- Boat outings
- Ski trips
- Theater events
- Manicure parties
- Health spa parties

REFERRAL EVENTS THAT ATTRACT CLIENTS AND PROSPECTS

As mentioned in Chapter 1, I advocate a client-centered approach to referrals. In most cases, you shouldn't ask for referrals based on "how I get paid" or in an effort to "help me build my business" (though that's a natural outcome). Usually, you should ask for referrals as a way to bring your important work (product and/or service) to others. The same holds true for referral events. When you invite your clients to bring guests to your events, do it from the perspective of bringing your important work to others.

For clarification, here's a sample conversation:

YOU: Bob, I'm calling today because I want to let you know about a fun event I'm hosting. Some of my clients have asked me to create an informal way to introduce myself—and the work I do— to some of their friends, family, and colleagues. We've reserved a special room at Chez Fancy next month, and we're calling it a "Chef's Table." The chef of Chez Fancy has agreed to come out of the kitchen and talk to us about the meals he and his staff will be preparing for us and then talk with us several other times during the meal. Those who wish to take a brief tour of the kitchen will be welcome to do so. It should be a pretty special event, don't you think?

BOB: My wife would love this . . . and so would I, for that matter. How do I sign up?

YOU: Well, here's the deal. This event is an opportunity for my clients who find value in the work I've done for them to introduce me to others. There will be no sales pitch whatsoever. I won't even talk about my business, unless someone brings it up one on one. We'll just have some fun, and perhaps I'll earn the right to follow up with some of the guests to see if they might be interested in allowing me to be a resource for them, as I have been for you. Does that make sense?

BOB: So you want me to bring a guest—a couple, I assume—who might enjoy the event and also want to meet you?

YOU: That's correct. Is this something you and HelenAnn would like to do? If so, whom do you think you might like to invite?

BOB: Well, I'm not sure. I'd like to talk it over with HelenAnn. Why don't you call me in a couple of days and we'll have it figured out?

It's as simple as that. You can print up nice invitations to this event as well. A key component to its success will be the personal conversations you have with your clients (over the phone is fine). Invite your "A" clients and don't delegate this phone call to an assistant!

THE CHEF'S TABLE

The example I used above is called the "Chef's Table." It's the kind of event that clients like to attend and to which they feel comfortable inviting guests. One of my large corporate clients has worked special arrangements with many restaurants across the country to support its salespeople in the field in this type of activity. They reimburse some of the sales reps' expenses, if (and only if) referrals attend the event.

As I mentioned in the previous example, chefs are usually involved in this event. Sometimes they prepare a special dessert just for the group. They also can recommend the best wines to go along with the meal.

If your event is in the evening, a guaranteed way to ensure that no one will ever forget the night is to have your guests picked up from their homes in limos or town cars. Talk about the "wow" factor! For a personal touch — and a nice excuse for getting back with your clients and their guests — take some photographs of the attendees. You might be able to hire a wedding photographer who would jump at the chance for some business during the week.

COME SKI WITH ME

David Vanderzee hosts a one-day "ski junket" at a local ski resort in the Northeast each year. Clients pay him back for the trip by inviting guests. David once told me:

I believe that the client relationship should be based on mutual trust and respect. To build that foundation, I think it is important to create an atmosphere where my prospects and clients have the opportunity to get to know me better. Sometimes I can best achieve this objective in a nonbusiness environment.

Being an avid skier, a natural forum for David has been a yearly ski junket. David hosts an all-expenses-paid day at a local ski resort, which enables him to forge friendships with many of his clients. In addition, he encourages his clients to bring guests, provide him with referrals, or both.

Although David picks up the tab for the day, his clients actually pay him back with referrals. They earn their spot on the trip by giving David five quality referrals or one live prospect. He sends a personalized letter to about 150 of his top clients. In the letter he explains that he's sponsoring the trip to thank his clients for their business and referrals throughout the year. He explains the "price of admission" as outlined above. He encloses a registration sheet for the clients to complete and return in a postage-paid envelope. This letter also explains that each referral would earn the client a ticket to a raffle for which the client need not be present to win. Says David, "This way, even those who will not be attending have the opportunity to give referrals and win some great prizes."

David hires a luxury bus, with a DVD player and a bar. The bus holds about 45 people (he emphasizes the limited space in his invitation letter). On the way to the resort they watch Warren Miller ski videos and his company's advertisements on the video. David says that "including the advertisements helps me deduct the trip as a business expense." Regarding the raffle, David says:

The prizes include a wide assortment of ski equipment, gloves, ski hats, poles, boots, bags, and more. Many of my clients donate items for the raffle, such as mugs and pens with their company logo. The donations keep my total cost for the raffle prizes down, while giving my clients the ability to promote their businesses to each other.

Not only does this event strengthen David's relationships with his clients, but his clients form relationships with each other. A kind of "fraternity" develops, made up of people who do business with David Vanderzee.

As you can imagine, a high-quality day of skiing is expensive—approximately $1,900 (probably more since my initial interview with him). According to David:

Personally, I don't think that one can put a price on the kind of goodwill I generate from this experience. Furthermore, hosting these trips has enabled me to build my base of quality referrals for future contacts.

David's clients know he expects referrals and that he will reward them generously. This is what I call a "referral mindset." This one trip generates referral calls throughout the year—prospects calling him. David estimates that the commissions he can directly trace to a single trip approach $50,000 or more. This isn't a bad return on investment, not to mention all the fun he has with his clients.

A SIMPLE DINNER PARTY

Andre Duffie is a financial advisor based in Wilmington, Delaware. Andre is fairly new to sales, but he's already doing things that top producers can learn from. Here's the story of Andre's first client referral event.

Andre invited his clients to "have a fun night on me." He also asked them to bring along any guests who might be open to learning more about the important work he does. Fifty people attended—45 clients and 5 guests. He fed them a nice dinner and then used a "clean" comedian as the entertainment "to loosen them up," he explained. (Smart move!) This was followed by a short talk on the state of the market.

Then came the *real* fun. Andre held a raffle for several gift certificates to a nice restaurant (the main prizes) and a few other fun gifts. Each guest was given five tickets for the raffle. Attendees were instructed to write the name of someone who might benefit from proper financial planning onto each ticket and throw it into the hat. The more tickets the guests threw in, the better their chances for winning.

The results speak for themselves. First, Andre received 65 referrals. Two months after the event, he had 10 appointments that yielded 7 new clients. Of the 5 prospects who attended the event, 4 became clients. But Andre's not done. He's still contacting the prospects and scheduling appointments. It's likely he will end up with 15 to 18 new clients from this one event.

Not only has this event enhanced his client relationships (they had a lot of fun), it worked to generate some great referrals. And if this isn't enough, here's the kicker. This event cost him almost nothing. How, you ask? He had five sponsors for the event; an attorney, a mortgage banker, a real estate agent, and two mutual fund reps. The first three are centers of influence to whom he has referred plenty of business.

From the numbers above, Andre knows that next time he needs to get more guests to attend. That's his highest payoff activity.

Now, let me say that this "raffle" idea does not work for everyone. You have to gauge your clientele. For instance, I ran into an advisor recently who held a pure referral event and did a raffle like Andre did. This event did not go over well with his clients and many of his invited guests. The feedback from the clients was that they already brought guests and neither they nor their friends appreciated the further solicitation. This was an important lesson. So, whatever you do, keep things very professional and always consider your clients. What you can or cannot do is primarily dependent on the relationship you have with your clients.

PARTY OF THE YEAR

Jeff Chaddock is based in the Midwest. He hosts what I call "The Party of the Year" at his home every year. He gets a big tent, hires a band, a comedian, and so on. His clients bring guests. And many of these guests turn into clients.

Jeff told me that some of his colleagues scoff at this idea. They think that he is only doing this out of ego—because he can afford it. Jeff also told me they can scoff all they want. This is a money maker for him in the sense that it cements the loyalty of his current clients and produces new clients every time.

Keep in mind that Jeff didn't start off with such a big event. He started small and grew the event as his business grew. If you are on a limited budget, you too can start small. The event will help you grow your business and your budget for the next event. If done well, each year will be a little bigger (more successful) than the year before.

LET'S TAKE A BOAT RIDE

I know a small business owner who uses his boat all summer long as a way to entertain clients and their guests. Bring a guest and you get to spend the day on his boat.

Now what a way to have a fun summer, celebrate your current client relationships, and prospect for new business! There are two things I particularly like about "boat prospecting." First, it's a small group, so you get a lot of time with everyone. Second, you get to know clients and prospects in a way that has absolutely nothing to do with your business or their business. You go through an adventure together—especially if you do some fishing or other water sports. Adventures like these almost always increase trust.

TAKE ME OUT TO THE BALL GAME

If baseball is our "national pastime," then taking clients and prospects to a baseball game runs right along with it. Of course, this is also true for any other sporting event—such as football, basketball, hockey, soccer, and golf.

The goal of this kind of event—like all social prospecting events—is to get to know people in such a way that you earn the right to call them later. Don't bring up *your* business unless they do. Of course, you can always ask them questions about themselves, like how they got started in business, what their biggest challenge is, and so on.

For referral events (maybe not so much for client appreciation events), I think you should keep these outings to small groups. Traveling to the event together in the same car, van, or sports utility vehicle will make it all the better.

GOLF—A DRIVER OF REFERRALS

Jerry Grant not only loves golf, but he has many clients who enjoy the game too. Several times a year, Jerry hires a local pro (with a great reputation) to run private clinics for his clients. Jerry invites a few select clients to attend, and he encourages them to invite one "successful friend." The clients understand what Jerry is trying to accomplish (meet good prospects), and they enjoy the great golf lesson for themselves and their friends.

Clients and guests show up for a lesson—which they always seem to enjoy. Then they hang out for a while for some golf talk and simple refreshments. Two things happen from these clinics. First, Jerry's relationships with his golf-playing clients are enhanced. Second, almost every clinic results in one or more appointments with new prospects. Jerry tells me, "It's a small investment that produces great results and a fun time to boot."

I've seen people do this sort of thing at a club, a driving range, and even in a backyard. Sometimes they have a full-scale barbecue. Be creative and have fun!

John Powell is a Pittsburgh attorney concentrating in the areas of partnerships, business succession, and estate planning. It's my experience that most attorneys don't have strong and creative marketing skills. John is an exception. He says:

> I've created a way to combine my love for golf and market-ing with my need to expand my network and increase my number of professional alliances. In February 1999, I formed the "Professionals Golfing Tour (PGT)." The purpose of the PGT is for professionals such as attorneys, CPAs, financial planners, insurance agents, and other related professionals to join together for four golf tournaments over the course of a summer. No clients are invited. This is purely for professional networking and, of course, fun.

John's PGT is entering its seventh season this year. Here's an excerpt from his invitation:

> This is the "other tour" where the golfers *aren't so good*. The PGT is for you, me, and other business professionals who

hope to drive more than 200 yards and on a good day to have fewer than 40 putts.

Does this event yield more than a good time and the usual frustration that any round of golf will produce? "You bet," John says. He and his colleagues have formed relationships that have resulted in a great number of quality referrals over the years.

APPROACHING FRIENDS FOR REFERRALS

So, how do you approach friends, and others, about the work you do with the goal of getting referrals? One of the challenges is that they haven't directly experienced the value of your work. So basically, you are not yet "referable" in their eyes. How do you become referable with them?

Obviously, it would be great if they became clients of yours (if they fit your profile), but let's assume that's not likely to happen—yet you still want referrals from them. I think the best approach is to sit down with them, at a time and place that is most convenient to them, and let them know what you're trying to do. First, tell them you have some ideas for expanding your business and you want to talk to them about your ideas, and you *value* their help. If they don't think they'll be able to help you, assure them that they will. Of course, you may have to buy them a meal, or cover a round of golf—after all, you are asking for their help.

At your meeting, your goal is to demonstrate the *value* you bring to your clients. The best way to do this is by telling stories, sharing anecdotes, and providing case studies. Most salespeople overlook the effectiveness of stories, anecdotes, and case studies as ways to demonstrate the value they bring to the marketplace.

For nonclients to refer you to someone, they have to have a very clear picture of your product or service and really trust the value you bring. Tell these people about the process you put your prospects and clients through. Give them specific examples of how you've helped clients solve problems, prevent difficulties, and take advantage of opportunities. Always stress: problem-solution, problem-solution.

Then, you move into our VIPS Method™ for asking for referrals. Here's that process, with a little script attached to each step:

1. *Discuss the Value.* "George, are you beginning to see the tangible value we bring to our clients?"
2. *Treat the request with Importance.* "Great. With that in mind I have an important question to ask you."
3. *Get Permission to Brainstorm.* "I'm hoping we can take a few minutes to brainstorm about people you think should know about the work I do. Can we try that for a minute?"
4. *Suggest names and categories.* "For instance, I think your fishing buddy, Joe, might be a great candidate for the work we do. Could you introduce him to me?"

It's really as simple as that. The key is basing this on the value you bring to the table. To accomplish that, you first have to tell the "story" of your value. By the way, you will find that if you do a good job of relating the value you bring to your clients, it's very possible some of your friends, colleagues, and family members might want to become clients of yours, too (if they fit your profile).

APPROACHING SOCIAL ACQUAINTANCES FOR BUSINESS

I had a client in our coaching program who asked me, "I've been meeting some people for golf over the last few months. They're not close friends yet, but we get along very well. Some of them would probably make great clients. I'm not sure how to approach them for business. Any ideas?"

As with the previous question (and life in general), honesty is the best policy. The key is *how* you bring it up. In most cases, you want your approach to be soft. Let me give you a short script to illustrate my thinking:

> YOU: George, there's something I've wanted to talk to you about, but I've felt uncomfortable bringing it up here on the golf course.
>
> GEORGE: What's that?
>
> YOU: My company and I have been achieving some remarkable results with a variety of businesses the past couple of years. I suspect you might find us to be a great resource for you. I was hoping I might be able to approach you in a business mode to see if, indeed we have something of value to offer to you. May I give you a call at your office to start a business conversation?
>
> GEORGE: Sure. Here's my card. Tell my assistant that I asked you to call me. That will make it easier for you to get through to me.

You need to find the words that fit your type of business and that are most genuine for you. The key is to confess your awkwardness and desire not to "hurt" the relationship. Sincerity always opens doors more easily than some tricky technique.

LEVERAGE COMMUNITY SERVICE

My friend, Donna Robertson, is one of the top real estate agents in my county. Every year she's rated either one or two— among thousands. And all of her business comes from referrals. She hasn't pounded the pavement handing out flower seeds in decades.

I always like to hear how successful people started in their respective businesses. It's fun to see what they're doing now, but it's more interesting to see how they got there. One activity that ignited her rise to the top was her involvement in a couple of community service organizations. Donna told me:

> When they see how you behave in a position of leadership, they are attracted to you. They say, initially to themselves, "If she handles our organization like this, I want her as my real estate agent." If they have an immediate need for your service, they become a client. If they don't, they refer clients to you.

When you pick one or more organizations to serve, don't join expecting to get business. Join because you think they do good work and you want to be a part of that. Over time, take a leadership position. Demonstrate your intelligence, creativity, and work ethic. In time, people will be attracted to you and the work you do.

CATCHING ELUSIVE REFERRAL PROSPECTS

I've talked about client appreciation events, bring-a-friend events, and referral events. But what about prospect events? Here's an idea that you can use to catch those elusive referral prospects.

All those who prospect for new clients inevitably create inventories of prospects who have been referred to them, but they just can't seem to get the prospects to meet with them. Perhaps the referral sources don't have strong relationships with the prospects, perhaps compelling reasons haven't been created as to why the prospects should meet the salespeople, or perhaps the prospects just aren't ready to commit to serious discussions.

Twice a year, Paul Taylor hosts prospect events, where the only people who are invited to attend are the prospects he can't seem to reel in. No clients or referrals sources are invited, just referral prospects. The last event Paul hosted was a wine tasting party. He had about 20 prospects show up, and 7 of them became clients.

Why would these prospects come to such an event but not come in previously for an appointment? I've discovered that in many different industries, many prospects would prefer to meet the salesperson or business owner in a low-key, social way before they're ready for an "official" meeting. Once these prospects get to know you in a social setting—where there is no "pressure"—they feel more comfortable meeting about business.

Do you have a bunch of referral prospects who have remained elusive? Try hosting a simple social event.

Chapter 6

Plant Referral Seeds Now— Reap Referrals Later

Promoting introductions involves more than merely saying a set of throwaway phrases to your prospects and clients. You first plant a seed with a prospect or client, then you water the relationship with value and service, and then you fertilize it with trust. Sooner or later, the relationship blossoms and bears great fruit.

Basically, three things happen when you plant a referral seed and one thing never happens. First, you will never hurt a relationship by planting seeds (unless you just become plain obnoxious about it). Sometimes when you plant a referral seed, you merely do just that. You plant the seed, and results are produced much later. Sometimes the planting of referral seeds can enable you to gauge the client's feelings toward the referral process. You plant a seed and your client reacts in such a way that you can tell that he or she is not sure or comfortable with the concept. This is good information to know, for it will dictate how and when you ask the client for referrals later (if at all). Finally, if you get in the habit of planting referral seeds, you'll realize that there are many people out there ready to give you referrals; all you have to do is bring the subject up. Planting seeds can result in immediate referrals.

"DON'T KEEP ME A SECRET"

One of the most popular and most effective ways to promote the referral process with clients is to use the expression "don't keep me a secret." This is a simple phrase that will do several things and *not* do one thing.

First, saying "don't keep me a secret" to your clients will not strain the relationship in any way. They're not going to respond by saying, "I can't believe you said that. I want my check back!"

Here are three things that saying "don't keep me a secret" can do:

1. *It plants the seed for referrals.* You can say "don't keep me a secret" to a client today. Then, some time afterward, the client will be in a conversation with someone who should know you, and will know that you're open to that introduction.

2. *Sometimes planting referral seeds can act as a barometer to how open your client may be to a subsequent outright request for referrals.* If your client responds, "I'll certainly tell others about you," then you know you have someone who may be very willing to provide you with referrals when you ask for them. If, however, the client responds with a cringe or says nothing at all, you know you may need to wait a bit longer in the relationship to bring up referrals.

3. *Not all the time, but more often than you think, saying "don't keep me a secret" can turn into a referral con-*

versation right on the spot—sooner than you thought it might. I get anecdotal evidence of this happening on a regular basis. Here are two concrete, real-life examples.

"I'll Talk to My Sister"

Larry DeNoia is a financial professional who attended one of the several training sessions I did for his company. He used this expression within a couple of days of our program with great results. I'll let him tell this to you in his own words.

> I had a client in my office on a Friday morning. Near the end of the meeting I said to her, "I wanted you to know that I'm still taking on new clients and would appreciate your not keeping me a secret." She immediately thought of her sister, who in the past had been happy with her advisor. Something must have changed.
>
> At 6:00 p.m. that same evening, I received a call from her sister. She wanted to meet with me as soon as possible. At 10:30 a.m. that following Monday morning, she made a commitment to invest over one million dollars with me.
>
> This was the fastest turnaround from prospect to client I've ever experienced. It clearly pays to say "don't keep me a secret" to all of your clients!

"My Mother Is About to Sell Her Home"

Brenda Hill is a real estate agent who attended a program I delivered to a group of agents sponsored by a mortgage company. Brenda told this story to me.

> I was attending the closing for a client who I had just helped purchase a new home. As we were walking to our cars, I

asked him if he was happy with the work I did for him. I then said, "Well, then, please don't keep me a secret."

He told me about his mother who was thinking of moving to a smaller home. Within about six months of this referral, I helped her sell her $4.5 million home and purchase a "smaller" $2 million home. This was a huge commission for me!

Will saying "don't keep me a secret" always result in immediate and lucrative referrals as it did in these two examples? Of course not. But this simple little technique does work—sometimes right away and many times with a delayed result. If you get nothing else from this book, please take away this phrase. You can add it to handwritten notes as a postscript, use it on your voice mail, or even add it to your e-mail signature line.

"I'M NEVER TOO BUSY"

Here's a simple way to plant the seed for referrals with just about everybody. Say to them, "I'm never too busy to see if I can help any of your friends, colleagues, or family members." Of course, you will adjust this statement to fit your selling situation.

I want to point out two things about this statement. First, it is not asking for referrals, as many people mistakenly think it is. It is merely planting a seed. This statement has its place in your referral toolkit and can produce some nice results—over time. However, don't confuse this statement—or any seed-planting statement—with asking for referrals.

Notice in the statement above that I use the words *to see*. These words allow you to qualify your referrals. Now, if you're new to your business or don't care much about qualifying your prospects, you can leave out "to see" and say, "I'm never too busy to help any of your . . ." Or you can say, "I'm never too busy to meet with . . ."

On the other hand, if you're concerned about the match of the referral prospect to your business, then the words *to see* will help you with that. When someone suggests a referral, you can then say, "Tell me more about George. Let's see if it makes sense for me to contact him." Or, "Let's see if George and I are a good match for each other. I don't want to waste any of his time." Notice how these statements, and just about every statement I give you in this book, will be as "client focused" as possible.

"IF I RAN INTO A GOOD PROSPECT FOR YOUR BUSINESS, HOW WOULD I KNOW IT?"

Be it a prospect, a client, or anyone else, if a person is in sales or marketing, or is a small business owner, you can plant a powerful seed for referrals by saying, "If I ran into a good prospect for your business, how would I know it, and how would you like me to introduce that person to you?" Asking this question shows your willingness to give that person referrals. And it is a great way to get a referral conversation going—sooner or later.

Do you think the other person will be appreciative of your desire to make business connections for him or her? Of course. Will bringing the topic up turn into a referral conversation for you right on the spot? Sometimes. It's important that this not just be a technique that you are using. You must be genuinely interested in making connections for that other person—when the situation arises.

I used to just say, "If I ran into a good prospect for your business, how would I know it?" Now, asking this question is fine, and it promotes the process, but introductions and connections are what we all really want—not mere referred leads. So I now speak in terms of introductions and connections as much as possible.

Maybe this person sells helicopter parts and you never run into anyone who buys helicopter parts. No matter. Your sincere willingness to connect that person with prospects is what really counts.

"HERE'S HOW I'LL CONTACT YOUR REFERRALS"

One reason people don't give referrals is that they're unsure of how their friends or colleagues will be contacted. They wonder if giving out the names of their friends to someone will put their own relationships with them in jeopardy. However, implementing the simple technique below will allay their concerns and plant the seed for referrals at the same time.

This technique is best explained through a sample conversation.

> GEORGE: Martha, as we work together, I want to let you know something that might come up and how we'll handle it.

> MARTHA: (curiosity aroused) Okay.

> GEORGE: As I work with my clients, they often think of others whom they think should know about the work I do. I just want you to know how we might handle such a situation should it come up for you.

> MARTHA: That sounds fine.

GEORGE: I don't like to call people and take them by
surprise. I've found it usually works best when
the person I'm calling knows who I am and
why I'm calling, and is at least open to a brief
conversation. So, whomever you identify as
people I might be able to assist, I'd ask you to
contact them first. It's important for you to
know that I'll treat them like royalty and not
be aggressive with them. Whether I end up
working with them or not, I can assure you
that neither party will regret the introduction.
Does that sound fair?

MARTHA: Absolutely. In fact, I already have someone
in mind. Let me tell you about her.

TEACH PEOPLE HOW TO GET REFERRALS

Here's an interesting phenomenon that produces referrals for
many people. First, I'll explain how I learned about it, and then
I'll show you how you can do it too. My sole business is teaching sales professionals and small business owners how to get
more business through referrals. I even help large companies
establish strong referral cultures that reduce their client acqui-
sition costs and boost profitability.

One thing I discovered is that when you teach people how
to get referrals, they are quite willing to give referrals to you.
I get many of my referrals even before I deliver any value. This
phenomenon truly amazes me. Part of it has to do with the fact
that I'm usually talking to vice presidents of sales and others
who understand the sales process. The other part is that most

of my conversations with them revolve around the referral process. Giving me referrals seems to be a natural thing for them. Sometimes, when I call clients to debrief a speaking engagement, they ask me, "When are you going to ask me for referrals?" They expect me to ask them, and they're ready to deliver.

Now, how do you create the same phenomenon for yourself? It's easy. As you learn more and more about how to generate referrals for yourself, teach others what you know. In many cases, you'll have clients who need to know how to get more referrals for their businesses. What a great way to bring more value to those relationships—and in a way that has nothing to do with what brought you together in the first place. Share this book with others. Heck, buy them their own copies. Go to my Web site www.ReferralCoach.com. Learn all you can there, and share that information with others.

Mike Gorman is a financial professional who attended one of my referral training sessions. Mike's target clients are executives and top-producing salespeople in car dealerships. Of course, the best car salespeople don't need the random prospects that walk into the showroom (they call them "ups" because the less successful salespeople take turns being "up" for the next prospect). They work almost completely from repeat and referral business. So Mike bought 20 copies of my book *Get More Referrals Now!* (McGraw-Hill, 2004) to give to some of his clients. He even called our office to have me autograph the books—which I was happy to do.

Within weeks of handing these books out, Mike began to get calls from clients with referrals. He told me, "I had no idea what the result of this little investment might be. One dealership owner referred me to the owner of another dealership—whom I'd been trying to get take my call for almost a year. He met with me and became a new client on the spot. Many other new clients resulted from this as well." So, as you might imagine, Mike maintains a small inventory of my books in his office to give out to people when the times seem right.

BY REFERRAL ONLY

Joe Stumpf (www.ByReferralOnly.com) is one of the leading referral trainers in the real estate industry. His workshops and conferences make a real difference for many real estate agents and other business professionals. One of the things Joe teaches his students is to put the phrase "By Referral Only" on their business cards. I think this touch is brilliant. Think about it for a minute. Over time, the businesses with the most prestige usually work "by referral only." You have to be introduced to them to get in the door. What a great position to be in.

When I was young, my family used to spend part of our summer at a mountain resort called Capon Springs & Farms in West Virginia. I have very fond memories of our summers there. One thing I remember is that you couldn't make a reservation unless you were referred by someone who had already stayed there. You had to be "introduced."

I grew up in a very middle class home. There was nothing prestigious about my life. However, many of the guests at Capon Springs & Farms were members of Congress and other high-level government officials from Washington, D.C. Being part of this group, of course, made me feel important.

Try putting the words "By Referral Only" on your business card—and any other promotional literature you produce. "By Referral Only" lends a certain amount of prestige to you and your business. If prospects see your card, they'll say, "Do you think she'll have time for me?" Or "Will you introduce me to her?"

Can you do this even if you don't work exclusively from referrals? Of course. If anyone says, "Well, I didn't meet you through a referral," you can respond with, "Well, most of my business is from referrals from happy clients. I hope to serve you so well that you'd be inclined to introduce me to others."

Set your vision for a thriving referral-based business and communicate it to everyone. As you've probably already gleaned from this book, there are times to be subtle about this and times not to be subtle. Be creative and find ways to promote your referral-based business in the words you speak as well as on your collateral information (promotional literature and Web site).

Here are a few more phrases you might use:

- The highest compliment you can give me is the introduction to someone else you care about.
- Referrals allow me to serve you better.
- Help us help others.
- Share the experience.
- Everyone is talking about our company.
- Spread the word.

In his book *Creating a Million Dollar a Year Sales Income* (John Wiley & Sons, 2007), Paul McCord provides a nice little checklist for you to make sure that you cover all your bases with your referral promoting phrases. I don't recommend you put something referral related on every single item below. Be a little bit discriminating, or you will come across as too self-serving. Here is Paul's checklist:

___ Office voice mail
___ Cell phone voice mail
___ Business cards
___ E-mail signature
___ Flyers
___ Brochures

___ Web site

___ Stationery

___ Notepads

___ Thank-you cards

___ Invoices and/or proposal forms

PLEASE LET ME KNOW WHOM I NEED TO THANK

You can use your outgoing voice mail to stimulate referrals. Here's a simple thing you can say that will help you build your culture of working from referrals and introductions.

> Hi, this is Bill Cates with Referral Coach International. Please leave me a message at the tone. If you were introduced to us, please let me know whom I need to thank.

One of your goals is to have the referral process become a part of how you do business and to make sure all your clients know this. When you put this statement on your voice mail, you're letting all your clients know that others are not keeping you a secret.

This particular idea came about one day when I was walking through our offices and overheard my business manager, Karen Hood, speaking to a new prospect on the phone. She said to him, "By the way, how did you hear about us so we know whom to thank?" I thought this touch was brilliant. She thought of this on her own. I guess working in and around our referral system for several years, she started using her own creativity to stimulate referrals for us.

Of course, I immediately started teaching this tactic in my seminars and speeches. One company went so far as to ask all of its salespeople to start using this statement in their respective voice mail messages. It's not only good for the clients to hear, it's also good for the sales reps to do everything they can to engage in this process. Every little thing adds up to creating that referral culture everyone wants.

Now, don't limit this idea to your voice mail. Take a lesson from Karen. Any time you or a member of your company is speaking with a prospect over the phone, assume that that person came to you through a referral. Say, "By the way, who introduced you to us—so we know whom to thank?" Now, depending on the type of business you have, some prospects may say, "I saw your ad in the phone book" or "I looked up your Web site." No matter, you've still just promoted the concept of referrals and introductions with them. You can even say, "Oh, okay. Many of our clients tend to tell a lot of their friends and colleagues about us, I assumed you were referred to us. No matter, we'll take such great care of you—maybe you'll want to tell others."

HE'S IN A MEETING WITH A REFERRAL CLIENT

I was delivering a referral training program in New York City one day, and a member of the audience, Ray Monroe, a financial advisor, shared with the group what he did to stimulate referrals and introductions.

First, here's what Ray Monroe said to us:

> I was in a meeting with a new client, who had been referred to us. My assistant, Shelly, took a call from a current client who wanted to speak to me. Shelly said, "I'm sorry, Mrs. Gephardt, Ray is currently in a meeting with a referral client." To which the client replied, "What's a referral client?" "Oh, sorry," Shelly said, "A referral client is someone who comes to us recommended by a friend, colleague, or family member. Most of our new clients come to our practice in that way."

About two weeks later, Mrs. Gephardt called Shelly to say, "Hey, Shelly, I think I have a referral client for you."

Mrs. Gephardt's referral client did, indeed, turn into a client for our firm. So I thought, "How else can we turn what happened here into a more regular occurrence?" Now, when Shelly or I are scheduling an appointment with someone, the conversation will likely sound like this:

CLIENT: Can I meet with Ray next Wednesday morning?

SHELLY: I'm sorry, Ray has a referral coming into the office that morning. Would just after lunch work for you?

Here is yet another example of how someone has incorporated the referral process into his everyday language. Even if you can't do exactly what Ray and Shelly do here, think about how you can begin to incorporate similar language into your conversations.

TEACH PEOPLE HOW TO GIVE OUT YOUR BUSINESS CARD

Sometimes our clients ask us for some of our business cards so that they can hand them out to others. We also ask them to carry some of our cards. Here are a few ideas to make this old concept work better.

When you give someone business cards to carry, say something like this to them: "George, I want you to always have my phone number handy. If anything comes up about the work we've done that prompts questions, you'll always have my number with you. Also, here are a couple extra cards. If anyone asks you if you like the work we did for you, you can hand them a card and see if they're open to my call."

If, in your business, you deal with account numbers or customer numbers, you can write those special numbers on your card. Now it becomes an important document clients won't want to throw away. If appropriate, you can also handwrite your cell phone number on your card. This is an appreciated personal touch.

Now, let's say a client asks you for some business cards to carry. First, you want to find out why. Say something like, "I'd be happy to give you some cards. Do you have some specific people in mind you'd like to introduce to our work?" Obviously, if the client has some specific people in mind, you'll want to have a conversation about referral, explaining what needs to be said to those people to get them interested in what you have to offer.

In all cases, you want to try to remain proactive. Most of the time, when our clients give out our business cards, nothing comes of it. Nice gesture, no results. So when you give business cards to your clients for them to distribute to others, teach them how best to do so. Here are a couple of examples:

- "George, thanks for your willingness to tell others about us. That's a great compliment. I'd like to tell you what I've seen work best with this sort of thing."

- "Just because you give someone my card and suggest he or she contact me doesn't mean that that person will. I've found that people get busy, forget, or even lose the card. What seems to work best in my line of work is when I can reach out and contact the person—be appropriately proactive. When you give someone my card, do you think you can see if he or she would be open to my call? Let that person know that I won't be pushy. I just want to see if I can be the same resource for him or her as I have been for you."

DON'T CREATE COLLATERAL DAMAGE

Collateral materials is a fancy term for your marketing materials such as brochures, flyers, business cards, and Web sites. One way many of your clients may choose to introduce you is by first passing along some of your promotional materials to others (including sending them to your Web site). If your collateral materials are not up to the level of quality that fits your industry, they will do more damage than good.

If you work for a large firm, I suspect most of your collateral materials are well designed and well printed. However, if you ever develop any of your own collateral materials—because you're independent, branding your individual practice, or otherwise—then you need to make sure your collateral materials are of the highest quality you can afford. This is not an area in which to skimp.

It amazes me how business professionals do everything they can to portray their successful image in their dress, car, office furnishings, and the like, but turn stingy when it comes to their supplemental materials.

How your clients perceive you when they first meet you carries over to their willingness to refer you. Your dazzling personality and high-level knowledge may be able to overcome poor marketing materials, but poor marketing materials may make it tougher for people to refer you—especially your centers of influence. Your clients may love you, but they don't want to feel embarrassed referring you to others if they know your marketing materials aren't first class—or at least at the level necessary for your industry.

In our office, one of our standards is "choose in the direction of higher quality." We try to apply that to everything we do—including the design and printing of our collateral materials. If the choice is one color versus two color, we almost always go with two color. If the choice is two color versus full color, we almost always go with full color. We spend freely on high-quality laser and inkjet printers so that everything that leaves our office looks as nice as possible.

Make sure there is a strong theme of quality in everything you do.

CREATE GOOD CONNECTIONS

One of the best ways to start getting referrals is to start giving referrals. Become a connector of people. Pay attention to products and services that you trust, and refer them to others. Become a resource center for everyone you know—especially your clients.

It amazes me that so many people who want referrals for their own businesses are not willing to give referrals to others. How are you going to create a culture of people giving you referrals if you're not willing to do the same?

When you give referrals to others, make sure that the connections go through. Giving someone a name and phone number of a new resource is a nice gesture, but there is no benefit to either party unless they connect. Call the parties a few days later to make sure the connection has taken place. When you take a little extra time and energy to make good connections happen for others, they'll do the same for you. Voilà! More referrals!

"OUR WORK WILL REMAIN CONFIDENTIAL"

One fear that some clients have about giving referrals is confidentiality. Some clients are concerned that their friends or colleagues may learn about some aspect of their life or business that they'd like to keep mostly private. Take away the fear that some clients have by emphasizing the confidential nature of your work. You can also teach them who you serve the best at the same time (so they only give you the types of referrals you want.) You can accomplish this in a simple conversation that will place absolutely no pressure on them or on you.

Here's the sample conversation (from the financial services world):

YOU: George, I wanted to let you know about something. Sometimes my clients like to introduce me to people they think should know about the work we do. If this ever comes up for you, I just wanted you to know a few things.

First, the work we do is, and always will be, completely confidential. No one will ever learn about your situation from me, or vice versa.

Second, our business is geared toward very successful people like yourself who have saved and invested well over the years, but who need someone to handle all the details and keep things balanced. [You will insert your own profile in here.]

And finally, I don't like to surprise people when I contact them. Should you ever identify someone you think should know about me, I'd ask you to contact them first and gain permission for me to call them.

I'll keep you in the loop as to how we progress. And, most importantly, I will treat them like gold. I'll never pressure them or do anything to hurt my relationship with you, by hurting your relationship with them.

Does this all make sense?

GEORGE: Sounds good to me.

YOU: Great! Just remember I'm never too busy to see
if I can help anyone you care about.

There are a hundred ways you can structure this conversation. Make it natural for you. Take away whatever fear they may be feeling about giving you referrals.

THE LADY WHO LOVES REFERRALS

Diana Borrel is a top producer for her company; and she's done it with referrals. She does it with two main strategies that follow my system to the letter. First, she makes sure she does a great job for her prospects and clients—so she's referable sooner in the relationship. Second, she plants referral seeds like crazy. For instance:

1. Her business cards have the words "I love referrals."
2. Her notes have the words "I love referrals."
3. She tells people, "I love referrals."
4. She uses an audio business card that's titled "Referring to You." (On the tape she says "I love referrals.")
5. She's comfortable bringing up referrals, and she does it all the time.

The results have been nothing short of fantastic. She discovered what I've been teaching for years—just planting the seeds can prompt many prospects and clients to give referrals without your even asking.

Many people love Diana's style, but it may not be *your* style. No matter. Just find a way to keep the referral conversation lively, without becoming obnoxious.

SHARE YOUR VISION FOR YOUR REFERRAL-BASED BUSINESS AND HOW YOUR CLIENTS BENEFIT

Do your clients even know that you are taking on new business and that it is good for you and for them if you can do so by virtue of their introductions? You know, many clients think— erroneously—that if they introduce you to others, you'll have less time for them. But they're wrong, aren't they?

It's important that all your major clients understand how they benefit from introducing you to others. Like many of the techniques in this book, this one is best illustrated through a sample conversation.

GEORGE: Martha, I wanted to tell you about a decision I've made in how I run my business and how that might impact you.

MARTHA: Okay.

GEORGE: As with many businesses, I have to balance my time between serving my current clients and finding new clients to serve. Quite frankly, I'd prefer to spend most of my time serving you and my other clients—instead of making marketing calls, spending money on mailings, and so on. So I've made a decision to run my business exclusively from introductions by my current clients. Does that make sense?

MARTHA: Yes, in fact, I almost referred you to one of my colleagues, but I was concerned that if I introduced you to someone else, you might not have enough time to continue to serve me so well.

GEORGE: Actually, that's a fairly common assumption,
but fortunately, it's not how this actually
works. I think it's good for you to know that
when my clients introduce me to others, everyone wins. *You* win because you get a chance to
help someone you care about—and in a way
that will not take time away from your level of
service. *I* win, because I might obtain a new
client. And your *colleague* wins, because he
gets the benefit of the work I do and can meet
me in the most comfortable and trusting way.

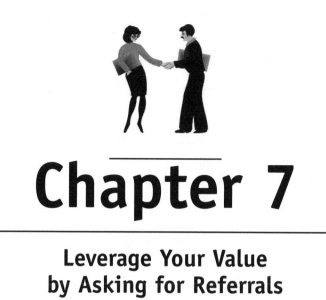

Chapter 7

Leverage Your Value
by Asking for Referrals

My hope is that you work very hard to bring great value to your prospects and clients and then you work hard and smart to serve them well. Now it's time to think in terms of leveraging that hard work and tapping in to the gold mine of referrals and introductions that is waiting for you. And I'm not talking about lopsided leverage. I'm talking about handling introductions in such a way that everyone benefits.

Over the many years of teaching referrals, I've witnessed many confident salespeople and self-assured small business owners turn into shivering bowls of Jell-O. This is where people begin to doubt themselves, their value, and their relationships. Of course, if you do many of the other things in this book, you will get more referrals. However, this chapter will likely be the most powerful one for you if you're willing to marshal your courage and act on these ideas.

HOW SOON IN THE RELATIONSHIP CAN YOU ASK FOR REFERRALS?

The most common questions I'm asked about referrals are: When do I ask for referrals? How early in the relationship do I ask for referrals? Do I ask on the first meeting? Or do I wait until I have provided some value, established my importance, to ask?

Can you ask for referrals at your very first appointment? Yes, but it's not always the best idea to do so. If your first meeting is filled with value for the prospect—real, tangible value—and the prospect generally has an open personality, then you can probably do it without fear of seeming too pushy.

Here's a formula that many sales professionals and small business owners find works very well for them.

First Appointment

1. Provide great value.
2. Make sure the value is recognized by the prospect or client.
3. Plant a seed for referrals like "I'm never too busy to see if I can help others whom you care about with this important work."

Second Appointment

1. Provide great value.
2. Make sure the value has been recognized.
3. Plant a seed like "don't keep me [or this process] a secret."

Third Appointment

1. Yup! Bring more tangible value.
2. See if the value has been recognized and/or the relationship is moving on the right track.

3. Use the VIPS Method™ to ask for referrals (see "Use the VIPS Method™ to Ask for Referrals," below).

Each situation and relationship is different. Depending on value perceived by the client and the openness of his or her personality (or lack thereof), you may have to adjust this formula. However, if you have a systematic approach that you apply virtually every time, you'll have a steady flow of great referrals.

USE THE VIPS METHOD™ TO ASK FOR REFERRALS

Are you ready to learn the absolute best way to ask for referrals? One in which you won't feel like you're begging? And where you won't feel like you're pushing your client? Let me introduce you to our trademarked method called the VIPS Method™. Does it work every time? Of course not. But it works a lot of the time and never hurts a relationship in the least.

Think of the referrals you get as the very important persons—the VIPs—in your business. The following are the four steps in the VIPS Method™:

V = *Engage in a Value discussion.* Within every face-to-face meeting with prospects and clients check in to make sure they see the value of the meeting, your process, and/or your relationship. The context will dictate what this sounds like. Don't be afraid of a negative response. And if there is something negative going on, you need to know about it.

I = *Treat the request with Importance.* This request is important because you do important work and you can help others they care about. Treat this request with the importance it deserves in two main ways: (1) don't forget to ask or run out of time so you can't ask for referrals; and (2) convey your request with confidence. Don't be wishy-washy or apologetic. To run a better meeting and not forget, use a written agenda for all your meetings. Put the words *value discussion* on the agenda. A meeting managed by an agenda will yield more time, and the agenda item "value discussion" will act as a reminder and hold you accountable.

P = *Get Permission to brainstorm.* Get buy-in for the process. There are times to be assumptive in the sales and the referral process, but now is not one of them. Don't assume they'll talk referrals with you. See if they are willing to "brainstorm" or "explore." And make it a collaborative effort. Together you will think of others who should at least know about you.

S = *Suggest names and categories.* Don't wing it with your referral conversation. Come prepared either with some specific names of people to suggest or with categories of people and businesses for whom you do great work. I promise you, the more prepared you come to this conversation, the more confident you will be and the better will be your results.

It's a simple process, but it's not easy until you practice it a bit and gain confidence. Then it's simple *and* easy. Again, will you get referrals every time you ask? No. But asking can also be a great way to plant a referral seed that will produce results later. Here's the good news: you don't need all your clients to give you referrals. You just need enough of them to do so.

"I'M ON A MISSION TO SERVE"

There are many ways to employ the VIPS Method™ to ask for referrals. Over the years I've developed several books containing referral scripts to help people formulate their own words and conversations. Here's one example of how you can use the VIPS

Method™—done from the perspective of a financial advisor and the client. I call the following script the "Mission to Serve." Watch how it touches on each of the four VIPS steps.

> You: Martha, when we first met, I told you that one of the things you can expect in working with me is that from time to time I would check in to see how I'm doing—how we're doing. I guess this is one of those times. First, is there anywhere you feel I've dropped the ball? Anywhere I've not lived up to your expectations?

> Martha: Well, we did have that misunderstanding several months ago, but I'm fine with that now. It's not a problem. No, I'd have to say everything is as I like it.

> You: Well then, let's talk about that for a minute. Where do you feel the value has come so far in our relationship?

> Martha: Off the top of my head, I'd say several places. First, the process we went through to determine the areas where I was falling short with my planning and implementation. That was very enlightening. Also, you and your team are so knowledgeable and responsive. I always feel "taken care of" when I work with you guys.

> You: Well, Martha, I'm glad you're seeing the value of working with us. And, of course, I hope to continue to be of value to you for a long time to come. You know, if it weren't for George,

we never would have met. I guess we both
need to thank George.

MARTHA: I already have.

YOU: Great. You know, there are many people who
never do the important work you've just
done—even very successful people who you
think would have handled all of this. They
never take the time to get a clear picture of
their financial situation, and they neglect to put
the right strategies in place. This, as you know,
is a shame. They set themselves and their businesses up for trouble down the road.

I'm on a mission to reach these people. And I
value your help in doing so. I'm wondering if we
can brainstorm for a few minutes about who you
know and care about who just might benefit from
the work I do. Can we do that for a few minutes?

MARTHA: Sure. I guess so.

MARTHA: Great. We're just brainstorming here. There
are several places we can go with this. I recall
that last week you mentioned your former
partner in your last business. Are you still in
touch with him, and do you think he'll take my
call if you introduce me to him?

Asking for referrals is as simple and conversational as
the script just given. Find the words that work for you, but
make sure you don't skip any of the four steps of the VIPS
Method™.

HOW OFTEN CAN I ASK A CLIENT FOR REFERRALS?

Let's say you meet with your clients two to three times per year, or even more. How often can you ask them for referrals?

There is no pat response to this question. So much of the answer depends on the clients' willingness to engage in the referral process, their individual personalities, and your relationships with them.

Assuming they're open to referrals in general, you might ask them during every other meeting. At every meeting, you should always have a value discussion and plant a seed.

If the individual you are thinking of asking is more guarded, you might only ask once per year.

Whenever you ask for referrals subsequent to the first time, always make sure you refer back to what happened before—both the good and bad. Don't be a robot with this. Every time you ask a client for referrals, you should take a few notes as to what happened. Then, when you want to ask that person for referrals again, you can refer back to the previous time.

If your client was not open to referrals the first time you asked, the next time you ask, say something like, "George, I'm glad you continue to see the value and importance of the work we're doing together. When we met several months ago, I suggested we explore the idea of identifying some folks whom you think should know about the work I do. At that time, you didn't feel comfortable with that. I'm wondering, now that we've had a chance to work together some more, if you might be open to a little brainstorming. What do you think?"

If you're asking a client who gave you referrals in a previous meeting, the conversation might go like this (after the value discussion, of course): "George, I'm glad you continue to see the value in the work we're doing. As you probably remember, the last time we met, we talked a bit about some folks who you thought should know about the work I do. In fact, I'm now working with your old partner, Bob. I was hoping we could spend just a few minutes brainstorming again on who should know about me. I was giving it some thought and had a couple of ideas to run by you. Can we explore this for a minute?"

Again, the key is to not be a robot, but just to be yourself and have a genuine conversation.

THE 60 PERCENT RULE

Now everyone's numbers are different, but my long experience in teaching people how to boost their business with referrals has taught me something I call the "60 Percent Rule." It goes like this.

Twenty percent of your clients will give you referrals no matter what. Well, that's a slight exaggeration, but if you provide good value and service, there will be a segment of your client base that will give you referrals without your having to ask. These referrals, by the way, count. Just about everybody I know should be getting referrals without asking for them.

Twenty percent of your clients will never give you referrals no matter what. You could run into a burning building and save their children and they still wouldn't give you referrals. These folks, by the way, can still be great clients.

Sixty percent of your clients will have a referral conversation with you—but only if you bring it up. Some of these clients will give you referrals when you ask—on your terms. And some of them will do it later—on their terms. The good news is that they won't mind your bringing it up, and it will never hurt your relationship with them (as long as you use our VIPS Method™).

This 60 percent group is an untapped gold mine for most salespeople and small business owners. Most people experience a huge gap in their referral potential. If you've been in business for a while, it's time to be proactive and close this gap. If you're just starting out, don't let this gap happen to you.

Fun with the 60 Percent Rule

Here's how one successful salesperson applied the 60 Percent Rule to get a lot of great referrals.

In January 2005, I spoke to a group of representatives within a large bank. During the course of my talk I covered the concept of the 60 Percent Rule. I had the pleasure of speaking to this group the following year, in January 2006. One of the bank's reps came up to me and told me about the great success she was having and how she was using the 60 Percent Rule to her benefit. She wanted to know my opinion.

Before she told me her story, I said to her, "If it's legal, ethical, and moral, and if it's working, then it's a good technique. Now, tell me what you're doing." This rep, Cindi, said that this was one of her typical conversations to get the referral (of course, you need to adapt this to your own personality):

CINDI: George, I wanted run something by you.

GEORGE: Okay.

CINDI: A marketing expert in our industry told me that I should expect about 20 percent of my clients to introduce me to others, without even asking. He said that another 20 percent or so of my clients would not introduce me to others—they just don't do that sort of thing. And, he told me that roughly 60 percent of my clients would consider introducing me to others, but only if I asked. I'm just curious where you fit in those categories.

I believe that Cindi has discovered a brilliant way to ask for referrals that contains no pressure whatsoever. She blames it on me and the statistics.

What is a client likely to say in response? I see at least three possible responses:

1. "I've already told people about you."
2. "I'm probably in that second category. I've had some bad experiences with that."
3. "I'm open. What do you have in mind?"

WHEN ASKING CLIENTS FOR REFERRALS, REMIND THEM THAT YOU MET THAT WAY

As you ask for referrals, it's always very effective to remind your client that you met through a referral. It might sound something like this:

> YOU: Bob, I'm glad you're seeing the value in the work we've done together. You know, if it weren't for Mary, we probably wouldn't have met. I guess we both owe Mary some thanks.

> BOB: Yeah, I guess so.

> YOU: Now I'm wondering if there's anyone *you* would like to bring this important work to. Could we brainstorm for a minute on other people you think should know about the work we do?

Obviously, you'll need to adjust the words to fit the situation, your style, and your client's style. I want to emphasize that reminding your client that you met through a referral can be very effective. However, you do this at the beginning of your request to discuss referrals—*not* as a way to overcome a possible objection to this discussion.

TRAIN YOUR CLIENTS TO GIVE YOU THE RIGHT KIND OF REFERRALS

Do all your clients know whom you serve the best; who fits your business model and who doesn't? If not, you're likely to get a lot of referrals that don't fit your ideal client profile and who may not be candidates for your business at all.

In subtle and not-so-subtle ways, you should continue to educate your clients about your ideal client. This will help ensure that all the referrals you get are of the right kind. For example, you could say: "George, I'm glad you see the value in the work we've been doing. This is truly important work. I was hoping we could brainstorm to see if we can identify people who should know about the work I do and who are *a good match for our business*?"

Or you could say: "As we brainstorm, let's keep in mind that I'm not right for everyone. My business is geared toward a certain type of individual. Let me take just a minute to explain that to you."

Also, if clients give you unsolicited referrals that don't fit your business model, let them know what happened to the referrals they gave you and then refine their perception of the best client for you.

If you keep getting the wrong type of referrals, then you are not educating your referral sources.

ASK PROSPECTS FOR REFERRALS

I am often asked if it's appropriate to ask prospects for referrals. My answer is, "It depends on two things." First, what is the personality of the prospects? Are they open in their style of communication? Are they forthcoming with information? Or are they guarded and reserved? The more open a personality, the easier it is to ask for (and get) referrals.

Second, what are you asking for? If prospects haven't truly experienced your product or service, then your product or service isn't referable yet. However, if you have already brought value to prospects—through teaching, questioning assumptions, big-picture thinking, and so on—then you may already be referable. Ask prospects for referrals in the following manner:

> You: George, I understand that you want to think about your decision to work with us. This is an important decision. If I may ask you, of what value do you feel this appointment has been to you?

> George: Well . . . you got me thinking about my business from an angle I've never used before. You asked some provocative questions, and I need to really sort all this out.

> You: That's nice to hear. I'm wondering if you'd be open to talking a bit about some of your colleagues who at least should be aware of what we do.

When you ask for referrals in this manner and you make it about your process and not the end product or service, you'll not hurt the relationship and you will get some referrals from time to time. These aren't the strongest referrals possible, but they can still lead to new business. Gary Kaplan attended one of our Referral Boot Camps. He was new in sales and needed to generate as much activity as possible. So he started asking prospects for referrals whenever he felt he could. Many of those prospects led him to new clients. When these new prospects became his clients, the original prospects were ready to do business with him as well.

GO FOR HIGH-TRUST RELATIONSHIPS

I got this idea from a top producer at a seminar I delivered near Baltimore, Maryland. Kevin Taylor uses the following language when asking for referrals. As his clients begin to ponder those they think would benefit from knowing him, Kevin says: "As you consider your colleagues, think of those people who would take my call just because you asked them to."

This touch is brilliant. You don't want just a list of names. You want to be introduced to your clients' friends and colleagues—whose trusting relationships will open doors for you. You want to be able to borrow their trust just long enough to establish your own.

Make referrals fun and be yourself!

USE A HIT LIST

When you're brainstorming with your clients for potential referrals, one great technique is to use a hit list or target list. Here are some real-life examples of how people do this.

Janet Earls, a commercial real estate agent, compiles a list of similar businesses in her area or niche. She limits the list to about 10 or 12 names. She hands the list to the referral source saying, "Do you know anyone on this list who should know about our program?" She also asks, "Is there someone you know who should be on this list?" I'll add, "If you were me, who on this list would you be trying to meet?"

Jeff Schleine, who sells to residential clients, uses a reverse directory to look up the names of neighbors of the clients he's visiting. He then "feeds" the clients he's visiting with names to see who they know among their neighbors. Then he gets the clients' permission to use their names when contacting new prospects. Jeff says, "It beats waiting for the client to come up with a name."

STOP FORGETTING TO ASK FOR REFERRALS

Many people tell me they don't ask for referrals because they forget or because they run out of time. In most cases, I believe, the issue runs deeper than this. The truth is that most people feel uncomfortable asking clients for referrals. So it's no wonder they "conveniently" forget or run out of time. Why would they want to do something that feels uncomfortable? Well, we know the answer. It's important to step out of your comfort zone so that you can help more people and make more money. Here's a simple yet profound technique for making sure you never forget and rarely run out of time.

Virtually every meeting you conduct with a prospect or client should be run by a written agenda. Running a meeting from an agenda does a few things. First, it demonstrates respect for the prospect or client through your preparation. Second, a meeting that is run from an agenda is usually more purposeful and, therefore, more likely to stay on schedule.

Almost every prospect or client meeting agenda involves the value discussion (see "Use the VIPS Method™ to Ask for Referrals" above). When you have the value discussion written into your meetings, you won't forget, you'll treat it with impor-

.tance, and you'll have more time to engage in one. When the value discussion is on your agenda, you'll be held accountable to doing what you know you need to do. Now, you may or may not move forward with asking for referrals, but at least you'll hold the all-important value discussion.

Many of those to whom we teach our Unlimited Referrals® Marketing System elect to move their value discussion from the end of their meetings to nearer to the middle. Some even put it at the beginning. For instance, let's say you're having a meeting with an ongoing client—someone you've met with many times before. I see no problem in holding the value conversation at the beginning of the meeting. You can hold the value discussion to set a nice tone for the meeting, conduct most of the meeting, and then ask for referrals near the end. The possibilities are limited only by your creativity and willingness to engage in the process.

Let me repeat: By having a written agenda, you will be accountable for having a value discussion. The key here is to be consistent and manage your appointments so that you don't forget the value discussion and you don't run out of time for it.

CREATE A SPECIAL MEETING TO BRAINSTORM FOR REFERRALS

One way to have enough time to get a lot of referrals is to create a special meeting just to do the brainstorming. You'll likely be surprised at how many clients will be willing to do this for you. I worked with one company where it was standard procedure for the sales reps to take the clients out to a thank-you lunch after some work was performed for them. At that lunch, they would debrief their most recent work and talk about the value of their relationship. Then they'd engage the clients in conversations about introductions to others.

Luke Wiley is a financial advisor near Cincinnati, Ohio. He attended one of our training sessions and adapted our model to fit his style. After he conducts his value discussion, he then goes for permission to brainstorm for introductions. Once the client says yes to the brainstorm, Luke sets up a special meeting—usually a thank-you lunch or a phone call—to explore for introductions. Before the meeting he always sends a small thank-you gift with a note that reads something like, "George, I truly appreciate the opportunity to explore with you who else should know about the important work I do. Here's a small token of thanks. See you next Wednesday."

If you create any kind of special meeting, make it as convenient for your clients as possible. Even if they usually come to you for business, go to them for this meeting.

"I'M NOT COMFORTABLE GIVING REFERRALS"

When you take care to be highly referable and you ask using our VIPS Method™, you won't get a lot of objections. However, not everyone is comfortable giving referrals. One of the most common objections you might hear when asking for referrals is a statement such as "I'm not sure I feel comfortable with this."

Your very first step should be to—softly—explore your client's perspective. "Have you had a bad experience with something like this before?" People are not ready to hear your rebuttal to their concerns until you've demonstrated a willingness to hear things from their point of view first. Once you've done this, they'll be open to learning how you see things. Oftentimes a simple statement such as "tell me more about that" is enough to get them talking.

After you've done your exploration and demonstrated that you understand, you can share your perspective by saying something like, "What do you think it would take for you to feel comfortable with this?" A client may tell you it is necessary to have more of a relationship with you first. He or she may want to contact a friend or colleague first. Or, you should be prepared for a client to say, "I just don't give referrals."

One of the ways to reframe their thinking is to talk about how the two of you can craft a way that they would introduce you to others—in a way that feels comfortable for all concerned. Or maybe you're just not referable in their eyes, yet.

How you proceed with this tactic is very important. Come across as pushy and you hurt the chances for referrals later. Do it softly and no harm will come of it.

TEACH YOUR CLIENTS HOW TO TALK ABOUT YOU

How you talk about yourself and your business will determine—to a great extent—how your clients talk about you. How you define your value and talk about your value actually teaches your clients how to talk about you to others.

The master at teaching salespeople how to communicate their value is Leo Pusateri (www.PusateriConsulting.com) from Buffalo, New York. Leo says that there are seven important questions you must ask and answer about yourself and your business. And you must be able to communicate the answers with speed and confidence. He doesn't mean you must talk fast. He means you need to have the answers ready. You don't have to think about them. You're not, in Leo's words, "winging it."

Here are the seven questions of Leo Pusateri's Value Ladder. If you can come up with succinct and unique answers to these questions, you'll win more high-level clients, and your clients will know how to talk about you to others.

1. Who are we?
2. What do we do?

3. Why do we do what we do?

4. How do we do what we do?

5. Who have we done it for?

6. What makes us different?

7. Why should you do business with us?

These questions are a great template for any promotional material you create. It answers the questions your prospects want answered—even if they don't come right out and ask them.

One more important tip: make sure your answers aren't meaningless platitudes like "we deliver great service." Of course you do. You had better. Here's how I test promotional copy that I write. "Can anyone else say that?" I want my answers to be unique so that no one else could possible have the same ones.

COLLECT CONTACT INFORMATION LAST

One mistake many salespeople make when clients think of potential referrals is to go straight for the contact information ("What's his phone number?"). I highly recommend that you collect the contact information near the *end* of the referral conversation. When you go for the information too soon, you can often make the referral sources nervous. First, learn all you can about the prospects: their relationship to the clients, their personalities, what's going on that's important to them, and so on. Second, talk about what the introduction will be like. Make sure the clients are comfortable with how they will be connecting you to their friends or colleagues. Once the relationship stuff has been covered, you can ask for the prospects' contact information (phone, address, and e-mail address).

REFERRAL TIC-TAC-TOE

Here's an exceptional idea I got from Jeff Gerwing, Certified Financial Planner from Winnipeg, Canada, who manages financial professionals. I've started teaching this point in my workshops, and people are using it with great results. How come I never thought of this? No matter, Jeff did the thinking for us. According to Jeff:

> Once they have set the stage for getting referrals, I get my advisors to draw a tic-tac-toe symbol. As you know, it has nine boxes. When they brainstorm for names, they put the first name in one of the squares (but never in logical order). As they continue to brainstorm, they put one name in the bottom corner, one name in the middle, one name in the top middle. They continue dropping in names until they are done brainstorming. Once the tic-tac-toe is full, they can go back to the names and qualify them.

> I am not sure of the psychology behind this idea, but in my experience, clients seem to want to fill the whole tic-tac toe board once we start brainstorming. The process definitely generates more names than simply listing the names on a page from top to bottom.

> I was working with an advisor and we had just finished some planning work with a client. We pulled out the tic-tac-toe idea and dropped in nine names within about four minutes. Why stop? We proceeded to draw another tic-tac-toe, filled it, and drew one more. All in all, I received 27 qualified referrals during that meeting. You can't argue with success.

WHO GIVES REFERRALS AND WHO DOESN'T?

Some people operate under the mistaken assumption that "if I just give my clients incredible value and service, they will tell others about me." While delivering great value and continual service is a critical part of this equation, there's more to it. There are several ways to look at this situation.

First, a person's personality will play a huge part in the dynamic. People with open personalities will usually engage in the referral process much sooner and much more willingly than people with guarded personalities. With open types, you can ask for referrals sooner in the relationship and more often throughout the relationship. On the other hand, with guarded folks, it takes longer to establish the level of trust necessary for them to feel comfortable in the process. Also, while open types will likely let you control all or some of how the process proceeds, guarded types will want much more control.

Another factor at play is people's history with referrals. Obviously, if individuals have had a bad experience with referrals in the past, they will be more fearful to try again. When you sense uncertainty on the part of your clients to give you referrals, don't ignore it. Explore it. Be genuinely curious to know their perspective. Sometimes you can put their concerns to rest quickly, sometimes it takes some time, and sometimes—no matter how much they love you—they won't play this game. Please don't take it personally. It's their stuff.

BE CAREFUL PAYING FOR REFERRALS

I am often asked my opinion about paying clients for referrals. I think you have to be careful doing this. In some industries, such as financial services, it's actually illegal. Yet, in other industries, I've seen it work fairly well.

First, let's understand why people give referrals—most of the time. People won't give you referrals or tell others about you unless you're highly referable. They have to have seen the value you deliver, like you, and trust you. Then, they want others to experience your value. If they don't think you're referable, buying referrals will yield either no referrals or very poor referrals.

So, regardless of what program you might initiate to reward clients for referrals, you should always make the referral request based on your value, the client experience, and the like.

Nevertheless, I've seen companies employ client-reward programs that can produce results. After close examination, I've discovered that the reward isn't usually what generated the referrals. The reward program emboldened the sales reps to actually ask for referrals by giving them a little "crutch" of sorts. Then, when asked, the clients were happy to provide referrals. The rewards program was just icing on the cake to them.

One of the pitfalls of paying for referrals is that it can cheapen the referral process for new prospects. When they suspect their friends are recommending you because they will be rewarded for that, they can become suspicious. The trust that you hope to capitalize on can become diminished.

However, when it comes to strategic alliances who may not be your clients but who are always on the lookout for prospects for you, that's a different story. It's not uncommon to pay these people a "finder's fee" or reward them in some other way. I am not an attorney. Heck, I don't even play one on TV. That's why you might want to check with yours about this. Many states require certain businesses to disclose that they get compensated for their referrals. If in doubt, check it out!

On the other hand, I'm a big believer in sending thank-you gifts to people for their referrals. I'll cover this in more detail in Chapter 8.

ADOPT AN ORPHAN

In the insurance industry, as well as in others, when a sales-person leaves the firm, the client assigned to that rep becomes an "orphan." Particularly for new reps, orphans can be a great source of early business. But, can orphans lead to more clients?

Many years ago I took a position with a company selling computer-generated graphics. This was a time when computer-generated graphics was in its infancy. One of the attractive parts of this new job was that the owners said that they would give me some house accounts to help me get started.

What they didn't tell me was that they were giving me all the accounts that hadn't done business with them in several years. I wasn't just getting orphans. I was getting old, disgruntled orphans. Lucky for me, I had a background in customer service. I listened to their problems without getting defensive. I told them I'd handle things differently, and many were willing to give me a chance. That not only got me going quickly, I got referrals pretty quickly, too. They saw that I wasn't afraid to address problems head on.

The key to getting referrals from orphans, as from other clients, is being referable. Many orphans feel neglected by your company because they haven't had anyone paying attention to their needs for some time. So first you need to win them over. Provide value to them in any way you can. Earn their trust, and then ask them for referrals.

It is possible that your company has some unassigned orphans. Find out. Go help them and they'll help you.

THE FAMILY TREE

We have a referral coaching program that allows me (and my other Certified Referral Coaches™) to coach many salespeople and small business owners. Not only do I believe I bring them great value, I also learn a lot from them. Here's a great referral tactic from a financial advisor.

When you are meeting with clients, get to know their "family trees." Now, for a financial advisor, that would include their children, parents, siblings, aunts and uncles, and so on. But this technique is not limited to financial advisors. If you sell printing, you can find out where they used to work; how they found their current positions; associations they may belong to, and so on. I imagine that every business has its own form of "family tree."

Don't just *pretend* to care about their trees, actually care about them. Find out what they value in these relationships; past, present, and future. Learn how their family trees impact their decisions and how their decisions impact their family trees.

Physically map out clients' trees and show them to your clients the next time you see them. You'll be amazed at the interest they will show (make sure you have names spelled correctly). If you don't type this up in some way, they'll never see it and wonder why they even spent the time. When you brainstorm for referrals, you have the perfect place to start. You can say to them, "As we brainstorm, let's start with the people who are most affected by the work we've done together."

JUMP-START NEW SALES

Carl Seadale is an extremely successful sales professional in Providence, Rhode Island. He sent me this e-mail revealing a great referral strategy:

> Here's a referral method that's great for business-to-business referrals (as opposed to business-to-consumer). And it works great if you are trying to work a specific geographic area. On your way to your next appointment do a "stop by" at a business that is related to your field. What do I mean by this? If I

am a life insurance wholesaler, I stop by a property and casualty shop. If I sold picture frames I might stop by a hardware store (some of them carry such items). Maybe you just stop by and ask for directions. The point is I try to make a connection of some sort. I walk in and introduce myself. In some cases I actually get some interest, but if I'm lucky enough to get someone who is willing to strike up a conversation, I can actually get to the point of getting them to make a referral for me. I ask, "In your opinion, who in town should I be thinking about seeing?"

I'm not kidding, if you're in a new area and you do this, you can actually get someone to make a referral for you! If it's an area where people "know each other," you may actually find someone who's willing to call ahead for you.

I'm not recommending this as a steady diet, but it's a great way to develop your skills and get some business to boot. There are a lot of people out there who will have their day made if they get a chance to help someone else. And don't forget that works in reverse. Be especially helpful to your existing clients and prospects and they won't forget you.

ASKING FOR REFERRALS WHEN YOU'RE BRAND NEW

Building a thriving referral-based business takes time. But what if you don't have that much time? What if you've mortgaged your new sales career or business on credit cards and have to create a boatload of new business right away? Well, you can still ask for referrals, but your request will be a little less based on the value you provide your clients and more about them helping you to become successful. While it's usually better for your request for referrals to come from your value proposition, just plain asking for help works too!

When you're just getting started in sales or business, you want to make sure that everyone you know knows what you do and how you help people. Get good at understanding the value you bring to your clients and get good at communicating that value to everyone. Sometimes this takes time. You can't always do it in one sitting with an old buddy or friendly neighbor.

So to prospects, new clients, friends, and family members alike, you can say, "I'm trying to expand my business this year and value your help. I've found that most people would prefer to learn about me from someone they already trust. Can we brainstorm for a few minutes to see if you know some folks who should know about what I do?"

Of course, you'll need to reword this a little to fit your personality, clientele, and industry. However, the key elements in the above request are these: "I *value* your help" and "Can we brainstorm?"

TESTIMONIAL LETTERS AND BLURBS: THE FIRST COUSIN TO REFERRALS

One of the best ways to be introduced to prospects that clients refer to you is a client testimonial letter. In addition to the role they play in introductions, testimonial letters (and blurbs taken from them) can be used in all aspects of your promotion and marketing. I believe that anyone who sells anything needs to have a body of evidence that what they are selling is worth the money and that the person who is selling it can be trusted. Of course, referrals are a huge piece of evidence. The first cousin to a referral is a testimonial letter.

If a client sends you an unsolicited testimonial note or letter, you should get permission to use the letter or blurbs from that letter. When you *ask* a client to send you a letter, let that person know you intend to use it for some marketing purpose.

When do you ask for a letter? The same time you might ask for referrals—when *value* has been given and *value* has been recognized. When your clients say good things about you, your process, and/or your service, you can say, "I'm glad you like what I'm doing. Every now and then it's great to get a letter from a happy client; would you mind if we put what you just said in writing?"

When clients give you referrals, you can ask them to write a testimonial letter or a letter of introduction that you may use to "warm up the introduction." Sometimes I'll ask clients for a testimonial letter, and then the next time I do some work for them I'll ask for referrals, or vice versa. I don't usually ask for both at the same time, but sometimes clients offer.

The more specific the testimonial letter, the better. Rather than having someone say "working with George and XYZ Company has been a great experience" (which is certainly okay), you'd prefer the letter to say something like "Not only has George Smith been a pleasure to work with, but he also goes out of his way to help us. What I like about him best is his willingness to face problems head on and not run away from them. He's pulled us out of several—potentially costly—jams." You get the idea.

Can you control what goes into the letter? Yep! There are two ways to do this—I do both all the time. First, during the value discussion, take notes on some of the good things the client is saying to you. When you ask that client for a letter, you can say, "I know you're busy, would it help you if I roughed something up for you to tweak and give back to me on your letterhead?" The client almost always says, "That would be great!" Then, I craft a letter—in the client's own words—based on what he or she has just said to me. Sometimes my clients want to write the letter. If they do, I give them a sense of what would be best for me.

Dave Horton is a very successful salesperson, and he told me how he uses testimonial letters:

> I have my high-profile clients write me a testimonial letter. Then they give me a list of people with whom they have some influence. I send out the letter and follow up with a phone call. I've used this strategy for years and it's been very effective. With this strategy, I end up creating mini-niches. For instance, I had a prominent medical specialist write such a letter and then give me the list of his association of other specialists. Very powerful!

Third-party endorsements work. Whether you use an entire letter or just a blurb, leverage the goodwill you create with your clients in the form of testimonial letters and blurbs. Make it a habit, and you'll soon have dozens of great letters to share as "evidence."

DON'T JUST SAY IT, HAVE FUN WITH IT

While delivering my referral speeches, training, and coaching, I often hear various ideas and phrases from sales pros who have some success with referrals. Here are a few I heard recently.

- *Idea #1.* Brian Gossamer says to his clients: "George, let me run something by you. Who do you know that you think would benefit most from meeting with me, but you're just not sure how to make the introduction?"
- *Idea #2.* Jay Madison says to his clients: "As we brainstorm, I'm looking for about 100 names." (Client laughs) "You're right. Too many. How about five?"
- *Idea #3.* As Laura Kreitzer is brainstorming with clients for referrals, she says to client couples, "If the two of

you were getting married again (couple laughs), who would you invite to your wedding?"

- *Idea #4.* Mark Hood says to his male clients, "If I gave you four great tickets to the Super Bowl, who would you invite—besides your wife—to go along with you?"

These are just a few examples. It's up to you to see how much fun and/or creativity you can put into your personal process for asking for referrals.

Chapter 8

Get Introduced and Show Your Appreciation

Before you and I were born—even before there was the telephone—people would work from "letters of introduction." You would get a letter of introduction from your friend, travel 1,000 miles to another city, and that letter of introduction would get you entry into peoples' homes and businesses. That same principle applies today.

In today's environment (do-not-call regulations, caller ID, gatekeepers, and the like), getting introduced in some way is usually necessary. Working from an introduction may be the only way to get your prospect's attention. However, having your referral source (nominator) contact the prospect on your behalf clearly has some risk to it. The prospect can say no, and your client may not know what to say to turn that person around.

ASSUME THE INTRODUCTION

When your client brings up one or more names of people you should meet, the first thing to discuss is what the introduction will be like. Be a little assumptive here. Say, "How would you like to introduce me to George?" If you have a favorite method (mine is e-mail), then suggest that. But, keep an open mind to other ways. In many cases, your referral sources will know the best ways to introduce you, based on their relationships with the prospects.

Once the type of introduction has been established, say to your client, "What do you think you need to say to George to get him to take my call?" Listen to what your client says. Work on this to make sure there is a compelling reason for why the referral should meet with you. But don't allow your client to make this product specific. What you did for this particular client may be very different from what you do for the referral.

Just as I believe asking for referrals should be a collaborative process with clients (and others), so too should the connection process. We brainstorm about who else we might be able to help. Then we brainstorm about how we get introduced to them.

This is an area where many people drop the ball. They get great referrals, but they don't use the referral source to help make a great connection. To use a football analogy, it's like driving 95 yards down the field to your opponent's three-yard line and then punting—not even kicking a field goal.

Ask for referrals with the clear intention of getting connected to your new prospects.

TO GET INTRODUCED OR NOT TO GET INTRODUCED? THAT IS THE QUESTION

As already mentioned, having an introduction to a prospect is a good thing. Once the nature of the introduction has been discussed and "negotiated," say to your client, "What do you think you need to say to George to get him to take my call?" Always listen to what your clients say. Work on this with them to make sure they have compelling reasons for why their friends should meet with you. But don't allow them to make the nature of the get-together product specific—unless you're just selling one product. What you did for a client may be very different from what you do for his or her friend.

One more great question to ask your referral source, "What's going on in George's life [or business] that's important to him?" The answer to this question can help you craft a good reason for why George should meet with you sooner rather than later. The more compelling the reason this prospect has for seeing you, the more likely it is that the meeting will happen.

DON'T TAKE REFERRALS THAT DON'T FIT YOUR BUSINESS

It's a very common mistake for people to think that they have to accept all the referrals that are sent their way. While this is an option, it is not the only one. Every business must decide on the criteria for what makes a good prospect or client. Generally speaking, you should not do business with people who are not a good fit. If they are not a good fit for you, then you are not the best for them. They should be working with a business that is geared toward them. It should be a win-win situation.

Now, some people decide to accept all the referrals that come their way out of respect for the referral sources. And, as I said, that's one option. And that's okay, as long as you are making that choice consciously, and not accepting bad referrals out of fear or awkwardness. Don't fear that if you don't take all the referrals that come your way, then your sources will stop giving you referrals. This is not true as long as you educate your sources regarding your ideal type of client.

Teach your clients and referral alliances about the kind of people you serve best—those who are the best fit for your business model. When you do this, most of the referrals they send to you will be good matches.

Whenever a source volunteers a referral for you, always qualify that prospect for your business. Say to the source, "Let's see if we're a good match," or "Tell me more about George. Let's see if I'm the right person for him."

If you are introduced to a prospect and you mutually determine you aren't a good fit, let your referral source know. You don't have to tell the client any details; you merely have to say something like, "George and I talked about his situation, and we determined I'm not the right person to be working with him right now." Or "George and I spoke and the timing isn't right for us now."

The best scenario is where you have already formed relationships with businesses similar to yours but that serve different segments of the marketplace. This way, if the prospect is not a match for you, you can still help that person by referring him or her to someone who is a perfect fit for the situation. In my own sales experience, it has always been easier for me to turn down business when I have someone to whom I can refer the business. In this way, the client gets served, and I put a deposit in the emotional bank account of a colleague or friendly competitor.

Lorna Riley, in her book *76 Ways to Build a Straight Referral Business A.S.A.P.!* (Off-the-Chart Publications, 2001), says: "Don't fall into the trap of saying yes to everyone. Avoid work that's out of your area of expertise, no matter how tempting it may be for you to maintain the illusion that you can do any- and everything."

GET MORE THAN A NAME AND NUMBER

When gaining referrals, don't just settle for a name and phone number. Whoever is giving you a referral is a tremendous source of information about your new prospect. Collect information that will help you to have a better phone conversation with your prospect and that will help you to create a more compelling reason for why the two of you should meet.

Ask the referral source questions to determine if the referral is a good match for you and your business. Ask things like "why did you think of her first?" and "I don't want to assume I'm the right person to be helping her; can I ask you a few questions about her situation to make sure I don't waste her time?"

Every business has a set of questions and answers that will turn a superficial referral into a great referral. You should spend a few minutes figuring out what information your referral source might be able to give you about the new prospect.

Here are a few generic questions you can ask:

1. How do you and George know each other?
2. What's George's personality like?
3. How do you think George will react to this introduction?
4. What's going on in George's life (or business) that's important to him right now?

Let's examine this last question—it's a very powerful one to ask. The client will tell you about some of the successes and the challenges that the prospect is facing right now or in the immediate future. From that, you can craft that all-important compelling reason for why the new prospect should meet with you right away.

Whether you ask for a referral or it's been volunteered to you, always use the referral source to research your new prospect. You'll be more excited about the call because now you're calling a "real person," and you'll have a more effective first call with the new prospect.

THE GOLDEN KEY TO INSTANT RAPPORT

When you call a prospect for the first time, sometimes the strength of the referral is enough to create a very warm call. Sometimes it isn't. Here's a strategy that can assure you establish instant rapport with almost every new referral prospect.

Find out what your referral source likes or admires (or respects or finds interesting) about his friend or colleague. Then use that topic in the opening conversation, if you can make it a natural fit. "Bob, you have a real admirer in Mary. She told me you have the highest level of integrity."

That compliment is a genuine one, and mentioning it shows your relationship to the new prospect's friend, colleague, or family member. Sometimes in conversations with clients this information will come out naturally, and sometimes you have to ask for it. Either way, when you get it, use it.

I remember when a client of mine introduced me to one of his colleagues. The conversation went something like this:

BILL: Ray, tell me something you admire about Mike.

MIKE: Mike has more integrity than anyone else I know. He's a real stand-up guy.

The phone call with Mike, later on:

BILL: Mike, this is Bill Cates, with Referral Coach International. Ray Vernon told me to give you

a call. I've got to tell you, he's quite an
admirer of yours.

MIKE: You can't believe anything Ray says.

BILL: Well . . . Ray said you have more integrity than
anyone else he's ever met. Those are the exact
words.

MIKE: Well . . . I guess you can believe a few things
he says.

Have fun with referrals and use the relationships to their
fullest potential. Make sure you're genuine in this strategy—
not just working a technique!

WOULD YOU LIKE TO INTRODUCE ME THROUGH E-MAIL?

E-mail can be a very effective way to get introduced to new
prospects. It works well for several reasons. First, it's very effi-
cient. Your referral sources can quickly send introductory
e-mails to their friends or colleagues. You can follow up quickly
after that. Plus, these days, people tend to respond faster to
e-mails than they do to voice mail messages. Second, it allows
referral sources to protect their relationships with their friends
and colleagues. I've written four books on referrals, and I love
to give referrals, but I will always send e-mails to my friends,
letting them know why I've given out their names. Most people want to "protect" their relationships, and e-mailing lets them
do that in a simple way.

Third, if you are calling people in their homes, you need
to be "do-not-call safe"—meaning you need to comply with the

National Do Not Call Registry. If someone is on the do-not-call list but he bounces back with an e-mail giving you permission to call him at home, you have a safe call.

As you and your referral sources are determining the best ways for you to be introduced to prospects, you might suggest that they introduce you through e-mails and CC (copy) you on the messages. When you see that a message has been sent, you can then follow up with the new prospect via e-mail, phone, or both.

To increase the likelihood of introductions being made, and to make it easier for your referral sources, you can e-mail "suggested" introductions for consideration. Of course, your referral sources can edit this introduction to suit their own style. Below are two introductions you can copy and paste into a file for easy access. You can adjust these introductions as you see fit and write a few more of your own. As you send them to your referral sources, insert your name in the appropriate places.

First, here are the three simple steps:

Step 1. Your client sends an e-mail to the prospect (a friend, colleague, or family member) and CC's you (a regular CC, not a blind CC).

Step 2. You wait between several hours to a full day before sending an e-mail to the prospect. Use your e-mail to negotiate a quick phone appointment with the prospect. You should also CC the referring client—at least on your first e-mail—so that the client can see that you have followed up.

Step 3. You call the new prospect at the appointed time. Or, if you never get a response to the e-mail, you can follow up with a phone call. As always, keep the referral source in the loop and send him or her a small thank-you gift with a personal note.

Here are a couple samples of e-mail introductions from which you can craft your own.

Sample E-mail Introduction #1

Hi George,

I'm writing to tell you about a financial service professional with whom I've been working. Monica Green has been helping me for about two months, and she's done some great work. We had some holes in our plan that I wasn't even aware of. She's creative and quite sharp.

I've given Monica your phone number and have asked her to give you a call. I don't know if you'll want to work with her or not, but I do recommend you take her call and chat with her for a few minutes. I think you'll agree that she knows her stuff.

Let me know how it goes.

Sample E-mail Introduction #2

Hi George,

I've been working with a very sharp financial service professional for the past few weeks and I really think you should meet him. Bob Smith is with XYX Financial Services and he's really gotten me on track. Through asking good questions, he discovered weaknesses in my financial program that my previous financial professional wasn't aware of—or didn't seem to care about.

Not only do I think you should take his call, but I think you should sit down with him and get a glimpse into how he works. I think you'll be impressed.

Either way, let me know how it goes.

SHOULD YOU SEND A LETTER TO WARM UP THE PROSPECT?

I am often asked about the value of sending a pre-approach letter to new prospects before calling them. People want to know if it will help to get their calls taken or if it will help to get the appointment and, eventually, the business.

My answer is always yes and no. Let me explain. I helped conduct a study with a group of financial advisors to determine the effectiveness of pre-approach letters. The finding was that a pre-approach letter had no impact on an advisor's ability to get an appointment or turn a prospect into a client. With or without a letter sent first, the results were virtually the same. However, many advisors felt more comfortable calling new prospects after having sent a letter.

Conclusion? If you suffer from call reluctance and if sending a pre-approach letter will help you get on the phone in the first place, then send the letter! On the other hand, if getting on the phone and calling the prospect is not intimidating to you, then forget all the fancy pre-approach strategies and get the process started as soon as you can.

One little comment about call reluctance. I understand what it is. I've experienced it myself. Get over it, get therapy, or get out of sales. You may think I'm kidding about therapy for call reluctance. I'm not. I've had a few salespeople tell me they've gone to cognitive therapists for help and that the therapy has worked.

A PROVEN STRATEGY FOR CONTACTING PROSPECTS

Once you receive a referral to a new prospect, there are many ways you can go about contacting that person. Here's a proven three-step process that will work with a variety of personality types and yield great results. I've been using it effectively for over 20 years.

Step #1: Call the Prospect

Instead of sending the "warning letter" that so many salespeople send, just get on the phone. Your agenda is to gain permission to send the new prospect a little information, and then follow up to discuss what you've sent. It's very simple. It's an easy yes for your new prospect.

Once the prospect agrees to receive some information, you say, "There's a lot of information I could send, but I only want to send what's appropriate to your situation. May I ask you a couple of *quick* questions?" Now you get to learn a few things about the person as it relates to what you're selling. In many cases, this questioning can turn into a great conversation that serves to move the sale along.

Most people will be fine with your asking a few simple questions. Make sure you use the language I just gave to you. It's been refined through many years of research and use!

The great thing that can happen with this situation is that as you have this little talk, many people will open up and give you some great information that will allow you to build trust and direct your conversation accordingly. Also, in some cases, the conversation will reach a point where you can go ahead and ask for the appointment right then to "deliver" the information in person or ask the prospect to come and visit you.

Step #2: Mail Them Something

In this situation, less is more. Mail the following to the new prospect: (1) a cover letter that addresses a few things you discussed on the phone and how you might be able to help the person in those areas; (2) some testimonial letters (or a sheet with blurbs); (3) one or two articles that you think the new prospect will find interesting or helpful (if you wrote the articles, that's even better); (4) brochures that relate to specific issues; and (5) a brochure advertising yourself or your company, if you like, but this is the least important item, in my view.

Step #3: Call Them Back

Call the new referral prospect back to discuss what you've sent and to gain the appointment. It's as simple as that!

The neat thing about this strategy is that if you encounter a fairly guarded prospect, you can begin to build the rapport by sending information. The prospect will like that approach! If you reach a very open person, you'll have a great conversation that might generate an appointment right away.

INCREASE REFERRALS BY HOW YOU SAY "THANK YOU"

I've seen two studies on the impact of sending thank-you gifts to clients who gave referrals. One life insurance company had 400 agents participating in its study. Over six months, half of the agents sent small promotional items to their clients who gave them referrals and the other half sent nothing. After the six-month period, the agents who were sending the small gifts had received 40 percent more referrals. Now, that's significant!

The other study was done some years ago by Baylor University. The study demonstrated an increase in referrals of 22 percent when clients were sent thank-you gifts. Either way, invest in your business and send small gifts to say "thank you" for the referrals people give to you. Don't wait for prospects to become clients. Reward the gift of giving the referrals.

Jeff Chaddock, an Ohio-based financial professional, gets more referrals than anyone else in his company of 8,000 advisors. How does he do it? He makes a big deal when people give him referrals. He sends small gifts such as certificates for an oil change, car wash, or movie. Or he'll send lottery tickets and other fun items that are inexpensive and easy to mail. When I interviewed Jeff for a magazine article I wrote some years ago, he sent me a Beanie Baby for my daughter. He's well known in his company for sending his referral sources big tins of cookies with his business cards and notes that read "share the cookies and share the cards." Every business is different. So what you do may be different than what Jeff does.

These days, almost every retail establishment has those plastic gift cards. Go to Starbucks, or Blockbuster, or Home Depot and buy 10 to 20 of them so that you always have them on hand. By the way, the more a gift is tailored to the interests of the recipient, the more impact it has. So tailor your gifts to the individuals.

I know one sales rep who had a coffee shop owner give him 100 coupons for a free cup of coffee—at no charge to the rep. The coffee shop owner knew that giving the reps these coupons would help attract customers to his new location. I know another extremely successful rep that made a deal with a taco place in her small town. She designed and printed the coupons herself, and the restaurant owner honored them. You may know business owners who would give you coupons for something free. Remember, don't make it a discount coupon—it has to be free!

Again, invest in yourself and your business. Giving small gifts to say "thanks" is not an expense, it's an investment. When you celebrate referrals by showing your appreciation for the new prospects, you get more.

GIFTS REINFORCE REFERRAL GIVING

Ken Horowitz is a financial advisor in New York City. Here's an e-mail I received from him recently about how he's creating success with referrals:

> Your referral system is great and has resulted in many new clients and a substantial increase in my yearly revenue. Per your suggestion, I've made a habit of sending a gift to everyone who gives me a referral. Clients appreciate the gift; they're flattered. It also reinforces the act of giving referrals and makes future referral conversations more likely to result in success. When a gift is something clients see or use regularly, like a pen, they will tend to think of you more often.
>
> I gave one client a "thanks for the referral gift" and he gave me 12 referrals next time we met for lunch. Another gave me a referral that led to a new client who was painfully underinsured and not managing his investments well. We help him and his family with life insurance, disability insurance, and investment strategies. My total compensation for all three categories totaled $62,000 for the first year. And of course, will yield income for a long time to come.
>
> Sending a small gift to say thank you for referrals can result in a huge return down the road.

STAND OUT WHEN YOU SAY "THANK YOU"

Tom Mays, a Florida-based financial advisor, reminded me of an idea I used to use many years ago. I guess it worked so well I had stopped using it for several years. Here's what Tom said:

> I give my clients a Thanksgiving gift instead of a Christmas gift. This year, I gave each one of my top 25 clients a pump-

kin cheesecake pie a day or two before their Thanksgiving dinner. I was the first one to send them a gift for the holiday season, so I know it stood out. This also prevents getting lost in all of the other Christmas gifts that get sent out. But here's the best part. They end up talking about me to others at the dinner table. I got tons of thank-you cards.

Did Tom get any direct business from this idea? Maybe, maybe not. But he sure created some goodwill and "business friendship" with his top clients. Ideas like this work to maintain client loyalty and earn the right to referrals.

GET CREATIVE WHEN YOU SAY "THANK YOU"

Here's what Janet Earls, with the Florida-based Sitkins Group, told me about how she uses gifts in the referral process:

> It's important to profile your clients and prospects to know more about them so that you can gift appropriately. When someone gives you one referral, send her one Tiffany wine glass (or beer mug). She'll keep giving you referrals until she completes her set. If he is a runner, send only one shoe from a pair of running shoes. Of course, he'll do what it takes (give you a referral) to get the other running shoe. The client will understand what you're doing and be happy to keep playing the game.

I've spoken to Janet about this, and she agrees with me that you cannot have this kind of fun with gifts with all your clients. You have to pick and choose who will respond positively and who won't.

One key principle regarding gifts that I've discovered is that the more personal you make the gift, the more bang you get for your buck.

Chapter 9

Create Your Networking Sales Force

Networking is not a one-time event; it's a process of meeting many people in many different types of venues and then finding ways to stay in touch with them in mutually beneficial ways. Networking is about giving value to others and getting value from them. It's not about just taking.

There are many great books on networking. This chapter is not intended to be a definitive work on the subject. I just want to give you a series of ideas and tactics to make your networking efforts more effective.

One principle of business that I have applied very successfully over the years is that of focus. I've found that the more focused my businesses have become, the more successful they've been. The same holds true for networking efforts. Be focused in knowing who you want to meet, why you want to meet them, and the best way to meet them. Don't have a network of people who know about you just for the sake of it. Be strategic. You'll maximize your time and energy by staying focused.

TAP INTO YOUR CONTACT SPHERES

Dr. Ivan Misner is the founder of a great networking organization called BNI (www.BNI.com). He has written several books on networking, and his company organizes networking groups all over the world. Misner writes about a concept he calls "contact spheres." "This is a group of businesses or professionals that can provide you with a steady source of leads," he writes. "They tend to work in areas that complement rather than compete with your business. For example, if you were to put a lawyer, a CPA, a financial planner, and a banker in the same room for an hour, you couldn't stop them from doing business. Each of them has clients or customers that could benefit from services of the others."

Misner shares some examples of contact spheres:

1. *Graphic communication businesses.* Printers, graphic artists, specialty advertising agents, marketing consultants. (I'll add paper salespeople, color separators, and noncompeting printers and artists.)

2. *Real estate services.* Residential agents, commercial agents, escrow companies, title companies, mortgage brokers, photographers, contractors, plumbers, gardeners, exterminators, home inspectors, florists, roofers, and even Realtors® in other towns.

3. *Contractors.* Painters, carpenters, plumbers, landscapers, electricians. (I'll add roofers, floor companies, and fence companies.)

4. *Business equipment vendors.* In telecommunications, computers, photocopiers.

5. *Special-occasion services.* Photographers, caterers, travel agents, florists. (I'll add musicians, DJs, bakers, event planners, tent companies.)

Corey Thomas is a sales manager for a small printing company in Maryland. One of its products is business forms. Corey has formed referral alliances with other commercial printers. When his printer alliances run across a customer or prospect who needs forms, they always refer Corey. Even though Corey's company can do some of the other types of printing, these referral alliances trust him not to go after their commercial business.

Have I touched on any area of yours? If not, think of other types of businesses that complement yours. How can you begin to ally yourself with others?

When I was giving a presentation in Greensboro, North Carolina, I had arranged with an airport transportation service to be driven from the hotel to the airport for my flight home. Arthur Goodman, the driver, picked me up, and we got to talking. Arthur owns a business called Designated Driver. He and his drivers are on call to assist people who have had too much to drink and need a ride home. What is unique about Arthur's business is that he not only drives customers home but he also drives their cars home.

Arthur's business is booming because of his ability to form referral alliances. He has made alliances with bartenders, the ABC board, restaurants, police officers, and others. Each of these groups of alliances serves Arthur with referrals, and Arthur serves them too, by making their jobs easier. This can work for everyone who has something to sell.

MAKE THE MOST OF YOUR REFERRAL ALLIANCES (CONTACT SPHERES)

I call members of your contact sphere "referral alliances." Once you have established who is or should be a referral alliance, you must do some important things to make sure your referral alliances become a productive source of referrals for you.

First, You Must Find Ways to Serve Them

1. *Give them referrals.* Make sure you know exactly who would be good prospects for them and how they would like to be connected to those prospects.

2. *Help them solve problems.* Make connections for them in addition to prospects. Connect them with others who can help them in their businesses and even in their personal lives (when appropriate).

3. *Give them advice.* Most people resist unsolicited advice, so be tactful. It's possible to create relationships that allow for giving each other helpful advice and coaching.

4. *Be a good listener when they need one.* Everyone needs a few good listeners in one's life. Be one for others. Don't be in a hurry to pull out your "tool box" and fix. Just listen and then ask them if they want feedback.

5. *Find out what success means to them.* To how many people have you actually said, "What does success mean to you?" and then helped them achieve it?

Second, They Must Know Exactly What You Do and How Others Benefit

To get the most out of your referral alliances, meet occasionally with them to remind and update them about what you do, how you do it, and how others truly benefit. The goal here is to make sure that you are referable in their eyes and vice versa.

Tell each other specific stories about how you've served your clients. Tell them how you've solved clients' problems or come to the rescue for them. The more your referral alliances know about how you have saved the time or money of others, or how you have made more money for others, the more excited they can be when they refer you to new prospects. Get your referral alliances excited about what you do so that they can transfer that enthusiasm to others when opportunities present themselves. Get excited about what they do as well. Now you have a bunch of quality people bragging about one another to prospects.

Third, You Must Work Your Network

Dr. Ivan Misner says, "It's not called net-sit, or net-eat, it's called Net-Work, and if you want to build a prosperous word-of-mouth-based business, you must work. Find ways to stay in touch with your allies. Merely knowing them is not enough; you must nurture the relationships."

Put your referral alliances on your mailing list to receive all your promotional literature, newsletters, and the like. When you host parties and other events for your clients, invite your referral alliances. Whenever you run across an article on a subject that you know some of them will appreciate, mail it out.

Here's why your referral alliances will give you referrals:

1. You've served them well, and they want to pay you back.
2. They want to be heroes to one of their customers, clients, or associates.
3. They know that helping you will come back to them one way or another.
4. They truly want to contribute to your success because they like you and trust you.

TAP INTO YOUR NATURAL MARKET

There is a term used in the insurance industry called "natural market." Your natural market consists of your friends, family, people you knew growing up, as well as people who know you from some earlier time in your career. Many life insurance companies and investment firms won't hire new reps unless they have strong natural markets from which to draw.

Who is in your natural market? If you haven't done so already, I recommend you make a list of everyone in your natural market. Do these people know what you're doing now? Do they know about the good work you are doing? If not, perhaps they should.

Members of your natural market are potential clients as well as potential sources of referrals. To gain their business or to gain their referrals, they need to know about your value. Take your list and identify all the folks you could get a meeting or lunch with just because you asked for it. These are people who probably like, care about, and trust you.

Teach them about the work you do. Give them specific examples and tell stories about people or businesses that have benefited from working with you. Make sure they really understand your value. If they are good prospects for you, it will probably become self-evident quickly. And if they're not good prospects, get permission to brainstorm with them about who they think should know about you.

Some members of your natural market may take longer to come around than others. Remember, they know you from a previous time in your life. It may take them a while to realize how good you are at what you do.

EIGHT WAYS TO MAKE THE MOST OF BUSINESS NETWORKING EVENTS

Going to business events is a significant part of meeting good referral alliances—not to mention prospective clients. Here are a few tips to make the most of your networking events:

1. *Treat networking as a process.* While one event can be very fruitful, it's better to think in terms of the entire

process. There is a cumulative effect that occurs when you go to several meetings of the same group. While it's okay to have high expectations going into a meeting, it's important to understand that the real results may only come after several meetings.

2. *Have a strategy and goal for each event.* You'll likely achieve much better results if you think through what you're trying to accomplish before you go to any specific event. Strategize the event. Set a goal for yourself. And be open to unexpected opportunities.

3. *Go with the mindset of giving.* It's easy to spot "takers" at networking events. No one likes to give to a taker. Show up as a "giver," and you'll likely get a lot.

4. *Look for more than prospects.* Many people make the mistake of going to networking events only to meet prospects. While it's always great to identify new prospects, you should also go to events to meet two other types of people: (1) prospective referrals alliances; and (2) people representing products and services you can later refer to your alliances and clients.

5. *Take a leadership role.* When you find an organization you connect with, consider joining its leadership group. As a leader, you will learn more about all the members and be able to serve them better. And, they will learn more about you and be able to help you. If you do it right, people will see that you are the type of person with whom they would like to work and also the type of person they would like to refer others to. So, do a good job as a leader!

6. *Elevate the quality of your small talk.* Make your small talk more meaningful. Ask people about their current, biggest challenges; their latest successes; how they got started in their businesses; and other probing questions.

If you keep your conversations superficial, you'll never learn anything about them, and they'll never learn anything about you. Be genuinely interested in them and their businesses (the key word is *genuinely*).

7. *Introduce people.* Whenever you identify someone who you think should meet someone else, walk them over and make a strong introduction. Doing so serves both parties, and eventually, you.

8. *Identify and serve the influencers.* Every organization and every industry has key "influencers." These are usually the most successful people who have been around the longest. Not only can these people make strong allies for you and your business, but they can also help you identify other allies. They understand this process and will work it with you if you work it with them.

ACT LIKE THE HOST, NOT A GUEST

Although I can speak in front of audiences from 10 to 10,000, I'm shy when it comes to networking events and other gatherings. A trick I learned long ago is to act like the host would act and not like a guest.

Lorna Riley, in her great book *76 Ways to Build a Straight Referral Business A.S.A.P.* (Off-the-Chart Publications, 2001), provides a nice chart that brings this concept to life:

Guest	Host
Takes a passive role	Takes an active role
More reserved	More outgoing
Waits to be introduced	Takes initiative
Often feels awkward	Helps others feel relaxed
Waits to be approached	Initiates conversations
Waits for invite to activities	Helps facilitate activities
Stays in one place	Mingles, makes introductions

If you're at all shy at networking and social events, try acting like the host. Offer to assist the host. Work the registration table. Offer to be in charge of a particular activity. First, your help will be greatly appreciated. Second, you'll put yourself in a more visible position.

STOP USING ELEVATOR SPEECHES

"What? Stop using that creative little explanation of what I do that took me so long to figure out? Stop saying it? Why? It sounds so clever." This is the reaction I got when I first started sharing this concept. Let's pause for second. You know what an "elevator speech" is, don't you? You've probably been told you need a 20- to 30-second answer to the question "What do you do?"

Well . . . you do need to be able to tell people what you do when they ask (and sometimes even if they don't). The problem I have with what most "experts" teach about this technique is that the final product comes out much too cute or staged. I think we need to be "real." In the movie *Spinal Tap* David St. Hubbins says, "It's such a fine line between stupid and clever." I think that if you're not careful—if you don't have a real answer to the question "What do you do?" then you'll come across as . . . well . . . stupid.

A colleague of mine—and a good referral coach in his own right—Mark Delton with Touchstone Investments suggests that instead of using elevator speeches, we ask questions as a way of explaining what we do, which also allows our listeners to relate our response to their own experience. Here are a couple of examples to stimulate your creativity:

THEM: What do you do?

YOU: Did you know that for most people, there is a

huge gap between where they are financially and where they want to be some day? Well, I help people fill that gap.

THEM: What do you do?

YOU: Thanks for asking. If something unexpected were to happen to you, would your family be taken care of and would the transition be as smooth as possible? Well, I . . .

THEM: What do you do?

YOU: Have you ever had doctors give you sample packs of a prescription drug they think might be helpful to you—so you don't have to pay anything for it? Well, I'm the gal who makes sure doctors know all about the latest drugs available, and I'm the one who gives doctors the samples so they can help their patients, like you.

Set aside some time—with your team or staff—to figure out what questions you can be asking to set the right tone as you explain to others the work that you do.

SEVEN TIPS FOR CONNECTING WITH PEOPLE AT EVENTS

1. *Don't fire-hose prospects.* When you meet prospects, don't get overeager and dump information on them. Ask them questions. Get to know them. Be genuinely interested in them.

2. *Be an unselfish listener.* Don't merely wait for your turn to talk. Be okay with just listening.

3. *Maintain good eye contact.* The key to this is managing distractions. If you find yourself being distracted by other people passing by, move yourself or the conversation so that you can focus on that one individual.

4. *Manage interruptions.* Be careful about allowing interruptions. If someone who knows you well interrupts your conversation, be gracious and introduce your old friend to your new acquaintance. If you and your acquaintance are getting into a good conversation, you might say to your friend, "Brian, it's great to see you. I was just learning about Terrie's business. Tell you what, give me a few minutes with her, and I'll catch up to you. Okay?"

5. *Take notes on prospects' business cards.* Use business cards to jot down a few notes either about what they do or about what your next step will be. First, they'll see you are paying attention, and, second, you'll actually remember what was said and what still needs to happen. Have you ever gotten back to your office with a stack of cards and not remembered the conversations and next steps? Taking notes will fix that problem.

6. *Reconnect before you leave.* When it's time for you to leave the event, do your best to reconnect with new people you met. Reaffirm the connections as well as the next possible action steps.

7. *Keep your word.* If you told people you'd call them later (or whatever), then do it. All the trust you built up at the event can be lost if you don't follow up as promised. Good follow-up is the lifeblood of effective networking. Most people don't follow up after events. Why go to events if you're not going to follow up? It's wasted time!

THREE GREAT QUESTIONS FOR GIVING REFERRALS

Here are three great questions you can ask referral alliances and prospects. When the questioning is done well, not only will you be in a position to help them, they will usually be more willing to help you in return. There is some overlap in these areas, so you may need to adjust a bit in a real conversation.

Question #1. "If I ran into great prospects for your business, how would I know it and how would you like me to introduce them to you?"

Question #2. "If I were to introduce someone to you, whom I know you'd like to meet, what one sentence should I use to describe you and the way you do business?"

Question #3. "What do I need to know about you and your business so that when I'm talking to people, I will know if you should meet them?"

IS A NETWORKING OR REFERRAL GROUP RIGHT FOR YOU?

Most larger towns and cities have networking and referral groups where the sole purpose is to generate leads, referrals, and introductions from member to member. The best of these groups—as far as I can tell—is BNI founded by Ivan Misner (www.BNI.com). In most cases, these groups will take only one member from any particular industry. And the good ones really know how to give referrals and create introductions.

These groups are not necessarily right for all salespeople or small business owners. A lot depends on your market. One of the first things you need to do to evaluate if you should join such a group is to ask yourself, "Do these people meet my prospects through the course of their everyday business or personal activities?" For example, let's say you sell helicopter parts. I doubt you'll find a preexisting group that will be right for you. However, many people have had great success forming their own groups—with or without the help of BNI or other organizations.

For instance, Hillery Schanck is a financial advisor in the Norfolk, Virginia, area. Hillery worked with BNI to form his own networking group. Initially, Hillery looked for members whose work was directly related to financial services (a certified public accountant, banker, and so on). After about a year, the group decided it needed a larger critical mass of members and opened up the group to others. For years, Hillery's best referrals from this group came from a residential real estate salesperson.

Here are seven tips for making the most of these groups:

1. Find the right group for your business.
2. Talk about your business in terms of how you truly help others.
3. Be crystal clear about who a good prospect is for you.
4. Meet with members outside of the meetings—to really get to know each other and become more referable.
5. Go to give!
6. Think in terms of giving and receiving quality introductions—not just leads.
7. Give it at least six months. Sometimes your best referrals and introductions come when the members really get to know and trust you.

MEET AND SERVE INFLUENCERS

Every industry has what I refer to as "influencers." These are people who work within your industry or target industry, are active in the community, or in some fashion have high visibility and influence with others. These influencers can be a great source of referrals for you—if they know who you are and how you benefit others.

First you have to meet them. Here's a very clever way to meet influencers. Write an article, a booklet, or a book on a topic you know a lot about and to which these influencers might have something to offer in the way of wisdom or specific techniques. Quote them in this work. Make them look good. They will appreciate your doing so, and, during your interviews with them, you will learn a lot about different aspects of their lives.

Next, you want to find other ways to serve them. Perhaps you can help them with a community service or other philanthropic endeavor. Perhaps you can refer business their way or introduce them to other influencers who will bring them value in some way.

Finally, make sure they get to know you and what you do. After the article is published, you can offer to take them to lunch to say "thank you." This lunch is your chance to begin building a business friendship with them and make sure they know some things about you. Once you have served them in some way, most influencers will make it easy for you to talk about yourself.

GET REFERRALS FROM YOUR COMPETITORS

You have different kinds of competitors, don't you? There are some people or businesses that do almost exactly what you do in the same geographic area. Then there are people and businesses who are in your same field but with whom you really don't go head to head. These are the competitors who can be a great source of referrals. Let me give you a couple of examples.

One of my "competitors" is a great speaker named Bob Burg. Bob is an expert on referrals and wrote a book called *Endless Referrals* (3rd ed., McGraw-Hill, 2005). While on the surface, Bob and I would seem to speak on the same subject, we actually cover different aspects of the same topic. So, people who have had Bob speak to their group at one meeting can have me speak at the next meeting, or vice versa. Bob has actually given me several referrals that have turned into speaking engagements. And I, in turn, have referred hundreds, if not thousands, of people to his book.

Kelly is a printing salesperson in the Washington, D.C., area who works for a printer with some very specific capabilities. He is always meeting and building relationships with other printers who are not direct competitors—either in terms of capability or geography. He prides himself on being able to give them referrals. They return the favor.

Make a list of all the "competitors" to your business. Now, look closely at the list. With whom can you create a friendly competition so that you actually find ways to help each other rather than fight each other?

Chapter 10

This Book Is
Worthless, Unless . . .

Now that you're almost at the end of this book, I thought I should tell you that all the ideas, tips, strategies, and tactics are worthless. Yup! That's right. Worthless. Unless . . . what? They're worthless unless you actually put them into action. How many books have you read, even marked up the pages with your own thoughts, and then never looked at again? I'm sorry to say, I've done that more than once. Oh, I act on my fair share of ideas, but I'm guilty of inaction from time to time—just like you.

Near the end of my seminars and workshops I often ask the question, "Is knowledge power?" The answer is always what you'd expect—a resounding yes. However, while I think knowledge is extremely important, it's not power unless you act on it. *Applied* knowledge has power. It's like the difference between potential energy (this book) and kinetic energy (you acting on the ideas in this book).

Ideas do not make you successful. Acting on ideas makes you successful. So, here are a few more ideas for you to act on—to make sure you put this book to work for you.

FIND A REFERRAL BUDDY

Have you been trying to build a thriving referral-based business for some time and have just not gotten as far as you would like? If so, here's an idea for you. Find yourself a "referral buddy" to walk this path together.

A referral buddy can serve you in so many ways. Perhaps the main way is accountability. I don't know about you, but as much of a "doer" as I am, I still slip on some of my goals—especially the ones where an extra dose of courage is necessary. I have long employed the concept of accountability in my life to make sure I do what I say I want to do.

For instance, I have a study group of other speakers and writers. We help each other formulate our visions for our respective businesses and then we kick butt to make sure we get there. I was struggling with making the time to work on a couple of important projects. So, I made the commitment to the group to schedule eight special days over the next quarter where I would work on nothing but these projects. For each day I didn't carry out, I would pay the group $250. At the end of the quarter I paid them $750. Now, the point of this kind of accountability is not to pay the fine; it's to make the goal. So, one of my colleagues, Steven Gaffney, said, "The fine must not be enough." And he was right. Obviously, it was easier for me to write the check for $750 than to follow through on what I said I wanted to do. So, we upped the accountability to $500 per day. Now, that got my attention! I have since formed a new habit because of this.

I was coaching a financial advisor in Richmond. Derrick desperately wanted to overcome his fear of asking for referrals. So we set a goal and created some accountability. Derrick is a long-time Republican. So, he wrote a check for $700 made payable to the campaign fund of a Democratic candidate in Virginia. He gave me the check and told me to mail it if he didn't make his referral goal for the month.

I have to tell you. I have never seen anyone create more referral activity in one month before or since. He was a maniac. He probably was too aggressive, but he learned how to pull back. It was a close call, but I didn't have to mail the check.

Who in your life can become your referral buddy? Who can you go through the learning process with? Who can you have hold you accountable and vice versa? This may be the most important tip you get out of this book, so please put some serious thought into this.

A DASH OF ACCOUNTABILITY

One of the best ways I know to change behavior is through accountability. Below is an example of some great results produced from just a dash of accountability. Imagine what you can do if you find a referral buddy or some other method to hold yourself accountable to new behaviors.

Justin is a sales manager who brought me to speak to his sales force. After the session he presented his reps with a simple follow-up initiative. For every rep who held 12 value discussions with clients within six weeks of our session, he would reward them with $150 in travel and entertainment money.

While many of the reps acted on various parts of the training, only 16 actually finished the full 12 value discussions. However, in about a 10-week period following the training, these 16 reps generated 132 referrals. That's what I call results!

This amazing success story speaks to three important points:

1. The value discussion aspect of my referral system is a very important and powerful tactic.

2. Doing something—anything—to increase the chances of implementation after a training session can go quite a long way.

3. The manager can have a substantial role in helping reps get more referrals.

If you are a rep—make sure you *act* on the ideas you like in this book. If you are a manager—please make sure you have some follow-up mechanism planned with all the training you do.

MY PLAN FOR REFERRAL ACTION

This is a tool you can use to ensure that you put some of the ideas in this book into action. First, make a rough plan of what you'd like to implement over the next four weeks. If you have some ideas you want to implement later, make sure you put them on your electronic to-do list so they pop up and remind you.

IDENTIFY AND CONTACT POSSIBLE REFERRAL BUDDY

I can say with utmost confidence that if you find a referral buddy, you'll produce even better results. This should be someone you trust to hold you accountable to certain behaviors and results. It's even better if that person is learning how to get more referrals too—so you can hold each other accountable for new results as well as brainstorm solutions together.

Week 1 _____ to _____

Enhance My Referability	Prospect for Introductions	Professional Alliances

Week 2 _____ to _____

Enhance My Referability	Prospect for Introductions	Professional Alliances

Week 3 _____ to _____

Enhance My Referability	Prospect for Introductions	Professional Alliances

Week 4 _____ to _____

Enhance My Referability	Prospect for Introductions	Professional Alliances

MY 21-DAY REFERRAL REINFORCEMENT PROGRAM

What you think about grows stronger in your life. If you think about referrals just a little bit each day, and then act on referrals just a little bit each day, you will create new habits. Here's a way to track your referral actions for about four weeks. Do something toward referrals every work day for 21 days, keep track of your behaviors in the form provided, and you'll be on your way to establishing new awareness, new habits, and new results.

Day 1 _____

Referral Activity	Why Significant	What to Do Better Next Time

Day 2 _____

Referral Activity	Why Significant	What to Do Better Next Time

Day 3 _____

Referral Activity	Why Significant	What to Do Better Next Time

Day 4 _____

Referral Activity	Why Significant	What to Do Better Next Time

Day 5 _____

Referral Activity	Why Significant	What to Do Better Next Time

Day 6 _____

Referral Activity	Why Significant	What to Do Better Next Time

Day 7 _____

Referral Activity	Why Significant	What to Do Better Next Time

Day 8 _____

Referral Activity	Why Significant	What to Do Better Next Time

Day 9 _____

Referral Activity	Why Significant	What to Do Better Next Time

Day 10 _____

Referral Activity	Why Significant	What to Do Better Next Time

Day 11 _____

Referral Activity	Why Significant	What to Do Better Next Time

Day 12 _____

Referral Activity	Why Significant	What to Do Better Next Time

Day 13 _____

Referral Activity	Why Significant	What to Do Better Next Time

Day 14 _____

Referral Activity	Why Significant	What to Do Better Next Time

Day 15 _____

Referral Activity	Why Significant	What to Do Better Next Time

Day 16 _____

Referral Activity	Why Significant	What to Do Better Next Time

Day 17 _____

Referral Activity	Why Significant	What to Do Better Next Time

Day 18 _____

Referral Activity	Why Significant	What to Do Better Next Time

Day 19 _____

Referral Activity	Why Significant	What to Do Better Next Time

Day 20 _____

Referral Activity	Why Significant	What to Do Better Next Time

Day 21 _____

Referral Activity	Why Significant	What to Do Better Next Time

Index

About the Author

Bill Cates is considered the foremost expert in referral marketing. He is president of Referral Coach International and creator of the Unlimited Referrals® Marketing System. For more information, visit his Web site at www.referralcoach.com.